"You asked the American people to help you get the government 'off their backs.' If the . . . people realized how rapidly federal government spending is likely to grow under existing legislated programs, I am convinced they would compel their elected representatives to 'get the government off their backs.'"

*—Commission Chairman J. Peter Grace;
letter to President Ronald Reagan,
January 12, 1984.*

The Grace Commission has given "a warning for the future. But you have also presented us with a program for action . . . lifting the economic burden already carried by millions of Americans who are overtaxed and overregulated by government."

*—President Ronald Reagan, to
J. Peter Grace and the
Grace Commission.*

"[The] onus clearly rests on the Congress. We have the full backing of the White House, but without an outpouring of support from the American people, the Congress is unlikely to take action."

—J. Peter Grace

A Taxpayer
Survey Of The
Grace Commission Report

William R. Kennedy, Jr.
Robert W. Lee

Green Hill Publishers, Ottawa, Illinois

We gratefully acknowledge the invaluable assistance given us in this project by our good friends W. Scott Stanley, Jr., and our editor Cynthia Ward and her devoted staff.

—ROBERT W. LEE
—WILLIAM R. KENNEDY, JR.

Copies of this book may be purchased for $1.95 from Green Hill Publishers, 722 Columbus St., Ottawa, IL 61350. (815) 434-7905.

Foreword

Big spenders in Washington may complain that President Reagan has "cut Federal spending to the bone." But in truth, the Grace Commission Report shows we haven't yet even trimmed much fat.

The Grace Commission Report follows up other pioneering studies of Federal spending like:

**National Tax Limitation Committee's book, *Meeting America's Economic Crisis*

**Don Lambro's book, *Fat City*

**And the Heritage Foundation's ongoing budget control studies, and many, many more.

But perhaps more than any other, the Grace Commission Report proves one thing true . . .

Federal spending abuses and runaway deficits will never be cured until Congress is forced, under our Constitution, to balance the budget and limit taxes.

With Washington dominated by powerful special interests, Senators and Congressman will not face the hard choices needed to cut spending, balance the budget and reduce taxes.

Right now, U.S. Senator Steve Symms (R.-ID) is trying to generate a national crusade to implement the Grace Commission's cost-cutting recommendations.

But for that crusade to succeed, we must seek first to enact a Balanced Budget/Tax Limitation Amendment to the U.S. Constitution. Backed by Nobel Prize economist Dr. Milton Friedman, this Constitutional Amendment will limit the growth of taxes and spending and force Congress to balance the budget.

Frankly, such an Amendment is essential to getting Congress to give the Grace Commission recommendations a full and fair hearing and implementation.

The next several years offer great opportunity for major restructuring of the Federal government. The Grace Commission Report gives us the roadmap back to fiscal responsibility — but the Balanced Budget Constitutional Amendment will pave *the road*.

Lewis R. Uhler
National Tax Limitation Committee

Table of Contents

Introduction

The spenders in Washington have said there is no hope. The line is that the only way to cut the federal deficit is to raise taxes. If those who hold that view controlled both the White House and Congress, more billions would be gouged from Middle Americans to pay for further expanding our welfare state. They say there is no alternative. Now we know they are wrong.

It seems that whenever America has faced a serious crisis some exceptional individual has stepped forward to remind us of our potential. In our current economic emergency, entrepreneur J. Peter Grace has been such a leader. Grace was appointed by President Ronald Reagan to head the Private Sector Survey on Cost Control. The Grace Commission discovered that more than $424 billion could be cut out of the federal deficit simply by eliminating waste and inefficiency from the national bureaucracy.

Thus, Ronald Reagan and the Grace Commission have given us a workable, humane alternative to raising taxes. The Commission did not attack the existence or substance of any federal program. It simply proposed that the government be held to stricter standards of efficiency, and that billions of tax dollars now being spent by Congress on wasteful programs be put to better use.

The Commission clearly warns us of what will happen if this waste is not cut. If government spending continues to grow at its current rate, our national debt will skyrocket to $13.2 *trillion* by the year 2000. That will be $18,000 a year, *in interest alone*, for each and every American taxpayer.

The fact is that we are quickly nearing the point of no return. The Middle American taxpayer has been called on so often to bail government out of its inefficiency and waste that he simply can't afford to give up any more of his hard-earned income. Most of the federal income taxes today are paid by those earning $35,000 or less. Indeed, when Middle Americans add up their federal income tax, state income tax, Social Security tax (with employer's contribution), as well as sales, property, and other ''item'' taxes, more than 50 percent of their income has most likely disappeared into the hands of bureaucrats.

In short, taxes can no longer fill the budget gap. As the Grace Commission demonstrates, the way to end deficits is to cut wasteful spending. The Commission's recommendations range from slashing telephone abuse in the Labor Department to making government power supplies more cost-efficient. We could save billions by privatizing some military and Coast Guard services which are either unnecessary or benefit only select groups of civilians. And reforms in accounting, debt-collection procedures, and government transfer payments could cut the deficit by tens of billions, simply by forcing government to abide by the standards of cost-consciousness and efficiency employed by private business.

Some would argue that the Grace Commission Report does not go far enough; that making the federal bureaucracy more efficient is not nearly as important as banishing government from competing with the private sector in such areas as commercial services. It has not been our purpose — or that of the Grace Commission — to discuss or dispute this argument. Certainly the Commission's work is an invaluable first step toward making government live within its means.

But even this step will not be taken unless you, the American taxpayer, understand what the Commission has done, and how *you* can help get the Grace Commission plan enacted into law.

Introduction

There are currently proposals in Congress to adopt some $100 billion of the Grace Commission savings. Whether these and other of the Commission's proposals are adopted will depend on you. So powerful are the special interests pressuring Congress to continue its policy of spend and tax, that it will take an equally insistent counter-force — the tax-payers of this land — to overcome those pressures and make Congress fiscally responsible. It's up to *you* to let your congressmen and your fellow citizens know that you *care* about federal deficits, enough to give public support to those congressmen who fight for the Grace plan — and public opposition to those who will not. This book provides ammunition for that fight. Don't listen to cries that it can't be done; the Grace Commission has shown that it can. But we must let our political leaders know that we understand the problem — and that we hold Congress responsible for the solution.

— **William R. Kennedy, Jr.**

CHAPTER ONE
Rehearsal

Huge federal budget deficits and ballooning government debt have raised widespread public concern. The man on the street is becoming more and more worried that the future of his children is going to be mortgaged to pay off government debts. Yet we're continually being told by our congressman that nothing can be done to cut spending without drastically injuring the poor and disabled. Well, now we know that is not true. Thanks to President Reagan, who appointed New York entrepreneur J. Peter Grace to direct a private sector survey on cost control, we now know how we can cut spending *without* hurting the truly needy. The Grace Commission has made some 2,500 recommendations which would carve more than $400 billion out of federal budget deficits in just three years.

The Commission's proposals are not only humane — they are *do*able. In fact, Ronald Reagan has successfully used such a report before. In 1967, while governor of California, Mr. Reagan organized a number of task-force teams comprised of leading businessmen. Their purpose was to scrutinize state government from a private enterprise perspective and offer suggestions for enhancing efficiency, cutting costs, and curbing waste. Those involved were requested by the governor to assume that state government was a company with which they wished to merge. What changes would they make? What business practices would increase the efficiency and effectiveness of state government? What existing government practices would be intolerable in a private business?

Some 250 executives contributed their time and expertise to the California project for nearly four months, eventually compiling about 2,000 proposals, of which some 80 percent (by Mr. Reagan's count) were accepted *and implemented*.

As merely one example of how the task force was put to

work, top hotel executives were assigned to inspect prisons and other state institutions. President Reagan recalls that "it was amazing the things they found that, from their standpoint and their expertise, could be done to not only improve the conditions, but improve them at a much lower price than the State had been accustomed to paying." There were, for instance, "fantastic savings just in such routine things as filing, storage files that weren't utilized but were stored in expensive, per-square-foot office space, when they could have been out in much lower-cost warehouse-type space." When one task-force member noticed that certain state employees were doubling over file folders to make them fit in the available file cabinets, he was told that state forms were printed in a size incompatible with the file-drawer dimensions. "Why's that?" he asked. "They've always been printed that way," was the response. So the executive, as described by President Reagan, "just picked up the phone and called the State printer, read the number off the top of the paper, and said, 'From now on . . . print those forms on' — and he gave them the proper dimensions. And that year, we bought 4,200 fewer file cabinets in California."

Governor Reagan was so impressed by the positive results of the California project that he resolved, as president, to launch a similar study at the federal level. That was the idea; now the president needed someone he could trust to make it happen.

CHAPTER TWO
The Main Event

At a press conference on February 18, 1982, President Reagan announced the formation of the President's Private Sector Survey on Cost Control. He named J. Peter Grace as chairman. Mr. Grace is chairman and chief executive officer of W.R. Grace and Company, a multibillion-dollar corporation with diversified interests in chemicals, natural resources, consumer services, and other areas. The firm operates in more than 40 countries of North and South America, Europe, Africa, Asia, and Australia. Peter Grace also serves as a member of the President's National Productivity Advisory Committee and is chairman of the Radio Free Europe/Radio Liberty Fund.

In 1980, W.R. Grace and Company sponsored a series of educational advertisements on television and in major newspapers, showing what was wrong with the Carter Administration's economic policy. "We could not," Mr. Grace asserted, "stand idly by in the face of bigger government and less and less private initiatives. . . . I felt we should do our part for the good of the general economy." During an interview with *The Review of the News* magazine in August, 1981, he declared: "Government is too big, too powerful, taking too much of our money in taxes, draining off our capital." There was, he said, "no doubt in my mind as to the long-range superior performance of an unfettered free market system over an alternative system closely regulated or 'helped' through subsidies and preferential treatment of selected sectors."

During his February 18, 1982, news conference, President Reagan pledged: "This is not going to be just another blue-ribbon, ornamental panel. We mean business, and we intend to get results." Special emphasis, he stressed, "will be placed on eliminating overlap, red tape, and duplication; identifying nonessential administrative activities; and increasing management effectiveness." He also predicted, "This will be the largest effort of its kind ever mounted to save tax dollars and improve the workings of government."

The Grace Commission was formally launched on June 30, 1982, when the president issued Executive Order 12369 to establish an Executive Committee and specify its mandate. Members of the Executive Committee were to serve without pay and the project was "to be funded, staffed and equipped to the extent practicable and permitted by law, by the private sector without cost to the federal government." And that, happily, is how it turned out. The time, money, and materials required to conduct the survey (total cost was estimated at more than $75 million) were provided at no cost to the taxpayer. The project was funded and staffed by the private sector.

If Peter Grace had any doubts about the difficulty of investigating the bureaucracy, they were short-lived. A delay of more than four months between announcement of the project and its formal launching resulted primarily from the very sort of government red tape and inefficiency which the Commission was assigned to expose. Those selected to serve on the Executive Committee had to receive necessary government clearances. In some instances, Grace's attempts to select the most qualified people ran into frustrating roadblocks. For instance, one major area for potential savings involves the upgrading of outmoded and inefficient computers currently used by many federal agencies. Mr. Grace thought, quite logically, that he should ask a top executive from IBM to chair the appropriate task force. But the bureaucrats said no. Such an appointment, they contended, would create a "conflict of interest." Mr. Grace also tried to assign an IBM executive to the Social Security Administration task force to work out changes in the outmoded Social Security computer systems, but apparently there were too many computers there, too, and the bureaucrats said, "no way." Eventually, Mr. Grace's computer specialist did find a place on the Commission — with the task force on Housing and Urban Development! Similar problems occurred in staffing the Air Force survey team.

During approximately 18 months of rigorous evaluation of the bureaucracy, the Grace Commission's 36 task-force teams, chaired by 161 top individuals from corporate, academic, and labor positions throughout the nation (and staffed by over 2,000 volunteers provided by those experts), compiled 2,478 separate and carefully-projected recommendations. If fully implemented, the cost-cutting and revenue-enhancing proposals described in 36 major reports and 11 special subject studies, could slash the federal deficit by a staggering $424 billion over a three-year period. By the time we reach the year 2,000, the *annual* savings could be $1.9 trillion! And it can be accomplished, declared the Commission, *without* "weakening America's needed defense build-up, and without in any way harming necessary social welfare programs."

The Commission's final report, marking the completion of its assignment, was submitted to the president on January 16, 1984, at which time Mr. Reagan promised "not just talk but aggressive action on your recommendations."

The overall prospects for success, however, will largely depend on the quality of the Congress we will elect this year. Since many of the suggested changes will require congressional cooperation, the road will be hard indeed if we make the mistake of electing yet another Congress dominated by big spenders determined to hamstring the Commission's proposals at every turn.

CHAPTER THREE
The Choice

Make no mistake: The way to cut federal deficits is through less spending, not higher taxes. Remember that we have been raising taxes since the beginning of the republic and we still have an unbalanced budget. Unfortunately, Congress seems unable to realize that Americans are already overburdened with taxes. As Chairman Grace noted in his report to the president summarizing the Commission's findings: "[M]edian family income taxes have increased from $9 in 1948 to $2,218 in 1983, or by 246 times. This is runaway taxation at its worst."

Mr. Grace also called attention to the important fact that "any meaningful increases in taxes from personal income would have to come from lower and middle income families, as 90 percent of all personal taxable income is generated below the taxable income level of $35,000." Indeed, there is little left to confiscate from the higher income brackets; even if "the government took 100 percent of all taxable income beyond the $75,000 tax bracket not already taxed, it would get only $17 billion, and this confiscation, which would destroy productive enterprise, would only be sufficient to run the government for seven days."

The basic choice is clear. We Americans *must* set aside our special-interest claims to government largesse, and unite as beleaguered taxpayers to demand cuts in wasteful spending. If Americans do not force Congress to cut spending by the end of this century, our country will be facing a crisis of such massive proportions that our cherished political and economic freedoms will likely be lost for generations to come.

If America continues down its present fiscal path, says the Commission, consequences by the year 2000 will be tragic indeed:

SURVEY OF THE GRACE REPORT

1. *Federal spending* will skyrocket to $1,703.5 billion annually. The Grace Commission proposals would save a full $535.2 billion.

2. *The federal deficit*, in constant 1983 dollars, would hit a monstrous $605.3 billion. The Grace Commission recommendations would cut it to only $14.0 billion — an improvement of 97.7 percent!

3. *Real economic growth* will grow at only 1.4 percent, versus 1.9 percent if the Commission's proposals are adopted — an improvement of 35.7 percent.

4. *Inflation* will average at least 8.5 percent — some believe it will go much higher — if things continue as they are. If the Grace report is adopted, inflation would be slashed to 7.3 percent, an improvement of 14.1 percent.

5. *Interest rates* will rise at least to 14.32 percent for three-month T-bills, and 14.75 percent for high-grade corporate bonds. The Grace proposals would cut these rates to 8.99 and 11.33 percent, respectively. In order for our economy to grow and prosper, business and consumers must be able to borrow money at reasonably low rates. If you've ever borrowed money to buy a car, a house, or to expand your business, you know there is a big difference between 14 percent and eight percent. The Grace Commission report tells how we can assure those much-lower rates.

6. *Industrial production* will be increasing by an average of only 1.4 percent if spending and taxation patterns continue. The Grace Commission plan would lift that figure to 2.3 percent, an increase of 64.3 percent.

7. *Real business fixed investment,* that infusion of capital into expansion that is so necessary to business growth and high employment, will rise only 1.5 percent under the *status quo.* The Grace Commission found a way to hike that figure by 60 percent, to 2.4 percent.

8. *Housing starts* will average 1,101,000 units annually; the Grace Commission program would lift them to 1,521,000 a year — an improvement of 38.2 percent. Combined with lower interest rates, that 38.2 percent increase would make it possible for many more Americans to own their own homes.

9. *Employment* in the civilian labor force will average two percent greater each year if the Grace plan is adopted.

There are courageous men and women running for Congress who will fight the battle for fiscal sanity in Washington, but they need a mandate from the people. As Peter Grace has said of his commission's program; the "onus clearly rests on Congress. We have the full backing of the White House, but without an outpouring of support from the American people, the Congress is unlikely to take action." This is a battle the taxpayers *must* win. To protect our own future and that of our children, we *must* demand that the federal government live within its means.

The wonderful thing is, the Grace Commission plan would move in that direction, *without* hurting those who are truly in need. In line with its limited mandate, none of the Commission's recommendations endangers either the substance or the legislative intent of existing federal programs. The vast majority of the Grace proposals would merely result in reduced waste; higher revenues from sources other than taxation (such as user fees); and a bigger cash flow made possible by improved management practices and more efficient operational techniques. Even so, adoption of these humane and sensible proposals would be a giant first step in returning this country to fiscal and economic stability.

CHAPTER FOUR
Waste Deep

Perusing the various Grace Commission reports is a fascinating, if frustrating, experience for the taxpayer. It is unlikely that another such extensive, thoroughly documented, yet remarkably lucid catalogue of the federal government's fiscal irresponsibility exists anywhere. So pull up a chair and relax as we continue our review of this parade of profligacy.

Foreign-Loan Subsidies *(Potential Savings: $360 million).* The Grace Commission discovered that taxpayers are subsidizing foreign borrowers. Interest rates in 1970 on Official Development Assistance (O.D.A.) loans, for instance, were 69 percent of the Treasury bond rate (the price at which the federal government borrows money). But by 1981, that foreign rate had plummeted even further, to a mere 27 percent of the T-bond rate. Which means, in the Commission's words, that "foreign borrowers were getting loans from American taxpayers at *2.5 percent.*" If the foreign rate could once again be raised to at least the 1970 average of 69 percent, taxpayers would realize a savings of $360 million — an amount equal to the federal income taxes paid by 162,308 median-income families in 1983.

Parole Review *(Potential Savings: $256,200 per year).* A prisoner who appeals an unfavorable parole decision is presently entitled to a two-step review of the decision. Incredibly, the same official who initially ruled on the appeal is also assigned to conduct the second review. In the eyes of the Grace Commission, this would make the first examination entirely redundant. Scrapping it would save an estimated $256,200 annually.

Abuse of Legal Services *(Potential Savings: in the millions).* The Criminal Justice Act authorizes free legal representation for defendants unable to pay the costs themselves. For 1981, the bill was $28 million. A judge's decision regarding a defendant's eligibility is based primarily on the (usually unverified) financial information which the latter supplies the court. One "unemployed" recipient of free legal counsel cited by the Grace Commission "turned out to own $4,000...in traveler's checks, two race horses, a pair of Mercedes and a motor home." It is difficult to know the full extent of this sort of taxpayer-funded rip-off, but it undoubtedly runs into the millions of dollars.

ACTION Agency Staffing *(Potential Savings: $26.7 million over three years).* The independent ACTION agency is the federal government's umbrella organization for sundry domestic volunteer activities. It was designed to advocate, promote, and support the voluntary efforts of citizens and organizations working to help alleviate problems confronting the poor, the disabled, the elderly, and youth with special needs. In the fall of 1981, ACTION carried through a 20 percent reduction-in-force (R.I.F.), eliminating 187 of its own employees from a total of 996. In 1982, when the Peace Corps was removed from the ACTION umbrella and made a separate entity, the ACTION staff fell by another 258 persons. Even so, the Grace Commission concluded that the agency is still heavily over-staffed and recommends that its roster be trimmed from 603 to 358 full-time and temporary workers. Although the cutbacks would entail significant percentage reductions in many areas, the Commission "firmly believes they can be accomplished without jeopardizing the agency's ability to fulfill its mission and carry out its programs effectively." Reduction of the ACTION staff as proposed would save $26.7 million over three years.

Parenthetically, in Fiscal Year 1983, ACTION incurred nearly $26 million in administrative costs while disbursing

$92 million in grants. That is a 22 cents-per-dollar administration expense — sharply higher than the 12 cents-per-dollar for administration spent by the private-sector United Way.

Annual Leave *(Potential Savings: $3.8 billion over three years).* The average private sector worker accumulates four days of vacation after six months on the job. In contrast, a federal government worker earns 6.5 days after six months, or 62.5 percent more than the private-sector worker. Adjusting federal vacation policy to fit the pattern in the private sector would save taxpayers $3.8 billion over three years.

Consolidating Air Traffic Control Centers *(Potential Savings: $418.4 million over three years).* There are presently 22 Air Route Traffic Control Centers (A.R.T.C.C.s) located throughout the nine Federal Aviation Agency (F.A.A.) regions. The 350 employees at the centers are mostly teams of air traffic controllers, and regulate traffic within specified geographic boundaries. Based on its review, the Grace Commission concluded that the number of A.R.T.C.C.s "can be reduced to no more than 15 using available technology and equipment." The change would reduce administrative and supervisory staffing by 60 people per center, while increasing operational staffing by 250 to 300 persons. The consolidated facilities would provide the *same level of air traffic control service and safety* and, over three years, would result in savings of $418.4 million.

Closing Air Traffic Control Towers *(Potential Savings: $59.9 million over three years).* The Federal Aviation Administration owns and operates 440 control towers at airports throughout the nation. The Grace Commission suggests that "it is feasible to close towers at many existing locations," since 57 towers have for three consecutive years fallen below F.A.A. retention criteria. The Commission notes that 3,208 of the nation's 3,648 landing areas do not have airport towers. And, 220 of those towerless air fields have scheduled air carrier service, including jets. "Yet," the Commission observes, "over 20,000 events occur per week at these airports, which nevertheless maintain an outstanding safety record and . . . [*handle*] other essential air services, such as weather observation. . . ."

Prior to the 1981 air controllers' strike, 184 towers operated 24 hours a day. At present, 87 operate 24 hours a day, while 97 get by on reduced hours. Also, some towers have been "defederalized" as communities have taken control, with no evidence of impaired effectiveness — and with lower costs.

Closing the 57 below-standard towers could save $45.4 million over three years. And, reducing operating hours of the 50 or 60 towers deemed by the F.A.A. to merit permanently reduced hours would increase the savings by another $14.5 million.

Cargo Preference (*Potential Savings: $15.6 million*). Federal law presently requires that at least 50 percent of the agricultural commodities sold or donated to needy countries by the United States under the "Food for Peace" program must be shipped on U.S.-flag vessels. During Fiscal Year 1981, $250 million was spent on the transport of such commodities. The Grace Commission calculates that eliminating the cargo preference requirement would have saved as much as $15.6 million, by permitting the substitution of foreign flagships for U.S. flagships and the consolidation of liner shipments on cheaper foreign-flag tramps, which are irregularly scheduled ships transporting cargo wherever contracted to do so.

Paper Shuffling *(Potential Savings: $7.1 million).* Big corporations can usually respond to correspondence within five days or so, even when the volume of mail is large. Not so in the federal government. Based on a sample of correspondence arriving at the office of the Secretary of Health and Human Services, the Grace Commission reports that "21 people...handle the drafting and clearance of a secretary-signature response" and, if you also include "typists, messengers, and other clerical support personnel," then the "actual H.H.S. number would increase to between 55 and 60." Sixty people to answer one letter! The Commission found the H.H.S. review process to be repetitive as well as inefficient, while the clearance process is "redundant, cumbersome, and time consuming." The "extensive time required and the complicated process involved in completing responses to letters received by the O.S. [*Office of the Secretary*] is symptomatic of H.H.S.'s organizational layering duplication problem. The numerous levels of review, the multiple clearances, and the delays in processing [*47 days is the average*], all indicate too many people with similar responsibilities performing the same function." If the handling of correspondence at H.H.S. could be brought to the level of most other federal agencies and departments, the three-year savings to taxpayers could total $7.1 million.

Disaster Relief *(Potential savings: in the billions).* Congress usually funds federal disaster relief programs *in advance*, with annual lump-sum appropriations going to agency disaster accounts. Such advanced funding does *not* earmark money for a specific disaster, so agencies may allocate the funds at their own discretion. In 1980, Congress reacted to the Mount St. Helens disaster in

Washington state with a $946 million relief appropriation. But, as summarized by the Grace Commission: "Due to the phrasing of the regulation . . . the money could be used in other areas. In fact, *only $386 million of the $946 million (41 percent) was spent on the Mount St. Helens disaster.* The balance of $560 million was spent on other disasters and could not be traced because it 'lost its identity.'" [Emphasis added].

Conserving Energy in Hospitals *(Potential Savings: up to $55 million a year)*. The Grace Commission referred to a General Accounting Office study revealing that private-sector hospitals used more than twice the number of conservation measures as are used in government facilities. "If federal hospitals were brought up to the standards of their counterparts in the private sector," the Commission asserts, "an estimated $16 million to $55 million could be saved each year in excessive energy costs."

Glut in Energy Department Management *(Potential Savings: $19 million over three years)*. The Department of Energy (D.O.E.) has twice the number of supervisors per employee as does the federal government as a whole (one for every three employees compared to one for seven government-wide). If that D.O.E. figure could be brought into line with the rest of the government, at least 120 unnecessary supervisory and management positions could be scrapped, resulting in a three-year savings of $19 million.

Consolidating the Federal Trade Commission *(Potential Savings: $1.1 million a year)*. Federal Trade Commission headquarters presently operates out of seven separate locations in Washington. In addition to the main F.T.C. building, there are six "satellite" offices scattered throughout the downtown Washington area. The closest is approximately two blocks from the main office, while the farthest "satellite" office is about 20 blocks away. The Grace Commission concluded that the "dispersed location of F.T.C.'s headquarters staff in seven different buildings . . . results in substantial direct and indirect costs."

There are, for example, added moving costs for transporting personnel, equipment, mail, records, etc., between buildings. There are added equipment costs when, for instance, the separate locations do not each generate sufficient volume to justify the purchase of cost-effective, high-volume copying equipment. There are inflated building-alteration costs, since, as the Commission points out, the "relatively small office sizes located in different buildings generally require higher alteration costs when changes are made in the nature or size of the F.T.C. programs." There are increased security costs (more buildings require more guards). And, there are increased leasing costs, since consolidation would result in reduced square footage — and costs — for the F.T.C. operations. Indirect costs include lower staff productivity and a relatively high turnover rate resulting from such factors as poor communication when face-to-face contact is not practical, the loss or delay of such items as records and files during transit between offices and inferior support facilities.

The expense of consolidating F.T.C. operations in two buildings rather than seven, as the Commission recommends, would preclude *immediate* savings; but over ten years the move would save an average of $1.1 million per year. Both the F.T.C. and the General Services Administration support the consolidation. It is now up to Congress to approve it.

Block Grants by Fish and Wildlife Service *(Potential Savings: $9.6 million over three years)*. Adoption of a block-grant program of aid to the states by the Fish and

18

Wildlife Service could save approximately $9.6 million over three years. Under the law, such savings would be passed along to the states. With a block grant, regional office staffs could be permanently reduced by about 150 people.

Fish Story. The Inter-Tribal Fish Commission of Portland, Oregon, had two exceptionally bountiful years for its catch of salmon before things returned to normal in 1978. The Economic Development Administration (E.D.A.), perceiving the drop from excellent to average, concluded that the Commission needed help, so responded with a $1.5 million grant to provide low-interest loans to "needy" Indian fishermen. According to the Grace Commission, "The money, spent on cars, furniture, watches, and other items, was only four percent repaid (principle and interest) by [*Fiscal Year*] 1982, four years after the grant was made."

Freight Discounts (*Potential savings: $530 million over three years*). The government presently spends $4.6 billion annually on freight, but does not negotiate volume discounts with suppliers. The reason? There is a serious lack of centralized freight information from the various federal agencies. The Grace Commission asserts that an "automated freight management system would save taxpayers $530 million over three years."

Job Overgrading and Misclassification (*Potential savings: $682 million a year*). Under the Government Service (G.S.) personnel classification system for the Washington, D.C. area, perhaps one-third of all positions are overgraded and nearly one-half, according to the Grace Commission, are misclassified with the wrong grade, occupation or title. Correcting the errors would save taxpayers $682 million annually.

Land Sales *(Potential Savings: $900 million over three years).* In 1964, 11.5 million acres of federal land were identified as excess acreage which could be sold off to the public. The Grace Commission estimates that $900 million in net revenues could be realized over three years from the sale of one-third (3.8 million acres) of that excess land. In turn, the influx of those new revenues would reduce service costs on the national debt by $146 million during the same period. Under the program, parks, wilderness areas, environmentally sensitive areas, and similar lands would not be subject to sale. The projected revenue and reduced debt-service expense combine to equal the total federal income taxes paid in 1982 by residents of (take your pick) Alaska, Maine, or Rhode Island.

Rate Inconsistency. The inconsistency of rate schedules among various federal agencies often leads one agency to pay far more for an identical service or commodity than another. The Commission cites an example where the "Environmental Protection Agency paid substantially more than the U.S. Coast Guard for the same services provided by the same contractor." The inflated charge, the Commission concluded, "was due largely to the different billing standards used by EPA and the Coast Guard. For example, the Coast Guard will pay $100 *per week* for the use of an office trailer. The EPA's schedule allows for $100 *per day*."

CHAPTER FIVE
Government Wealth Transfers

According to the Grace Commission, "'Welfare' was unknown in America before the 1930's, when the Roosevelt Administration introduced numerous public assistance programs in response to the Great Depression. The concepts initiated during the Roosevelt era have dramatically changed the relationship between the American people and their government, as evidenced by the enormity of the current 'welfare industry.'"

Enormity, indeed. The Commission cites figures for only ten of the 64 needs-based or means-tested programs which now exist. The total cost of those ten was $61.3 billion in Fiscal Year 1982. For perspective, it's interesting to note that the *total* federal income taxes paid in 1981 by all taxpayers in the nation earning under $20,000 was $50 billion.

There are two kinds of transfer payments: *Earned,* which include Social Security, the various Veterans Administration entitlement programs, and others which involve benefits paid on the basis of earlier contributions of time or money by the recipient; and *unearned,* which give tax money on the basis of need, or some means-tested qualification like income or assets. There are already more than 60 unearned-type welfare programs on the books. Their purpose is to transfer wealth from those who have it to those who don't. Though these programs were set up to help those who are not able to provide for themselves, welfare programs subsidize some who *could* work, but don't.

Most people don't realize it, but the Grace Commission points out that "100 percent of what is collected" in personal income taxes "is absorbed solely by interest on the federal debt and by federal government contributions to transfer payments. In other words, *all individual income tax revenues are gone before one nickel is spent on the ser-*

vices which taxpayers expect from their government" [Emphasis added]. There is enormous waste and abuse associated with the various welfare programs. Based on 1982 data, 6.3 percent of the total federal and state benefit payments for five major programs (Aid For Dependent Children, Food Stamps, Supplementary Security Income, Medicaid, and Section 8 Housing) resulted in overpayments, accounting for $4.1 billion in wasted tax dollars. This is the total federal, individual income and employment tax burden paid by residents of Arizona in 1982. The Commission also learned that overpayments under the Supplemental Security Income (S.S.I.) program for Fiscal Year 1981 "totaled more than $400 million, an *average overpayment* of $105 per recipient." The Grace Commission also reported that $4.1 billion in overpayments is expected to occur in just five programs. And it pinpointed almost $14.6 billion in unauthorized Social Security payments during Fiscal Years 1980 to 1982.

Verification of income is crucial to the responsible administration of transfer programs. It is the only way to be reasonably sure that assistance goes only to those the law intended to help. The Grace team discovered, however, that "present data sources are neither centralized nor consistent in availability." As a result of this lack of coordinated government information, vast amounts of money go to unauthorized and unintended recipients each year. For example, the Commission pointed out that the Aid For Dependent Children (A.F.D.C.), Medicare, and Food Stamp programs, which paid out more than $37 billion to 44.3 million persons in Fiscal Year 1982, require the maintenance of eligibility information on applicants and recipients. "There is," however, "no centralized data base to determine eligibility for public assistance for these programs. Income and asset information is not uniformly defined, and there are separately-formatted application forms for each program. Record keeping is not well-organized.'' Not only are a scandalous number of duplicate and/or erroneous payments being made to beneficiaries, but "extensive staff time is being spent on separate programs that require examination of the same or similar data and interview procedures.'' These wasteful and inefficient procedures are doubly hurtful to people; they fail to help those in need, and they drain private-sector capital that could be fueling business expansion and creating new, productive jobs.

To improve the incredibly lax verification process, the Commission would modernize the government's automated data processing capability, and require the submission of Social Security numbers and income tax returns before individuals can qualify for A.F.D.C., Food Stamps, S.S.I., Medicaid, and Section 8 Housing programs. A conservative estimate of the potential net savings is more than $2.2 billion over three years. That is equal to the total federal income taxes paid in 1981 by the combined citizenry of North Dakota, South Dakota, and Alaska.

The Social Security program made erroneous payments amounting to $14.6 billion between 1980 and 1982. Almost $1.3 billion of that was due to the failure of Old Age and Survivors Insurance (O.A.S.I.) beneficiaries to report their earnings. The Grace Commission learned that the system used by the Social Security Administration (S.S.A.) to enforce prompt income reporting "is three years behind schedule.'' That delay has cost the government $128 million in interest for Fiscal Year 1983 alone.

Right now, if you are denied benefits under the Social Security System's Disability Insurance program, you may appeal — and appeal — and appeal. At each of the three appeals, your case will be reviewed from scratch and weighed in complete independence of prior considerations. If you are not then satisfied with the decision, you may go to federal court over the matter. The Grace Commission learned that the rate of reversal by administrative law judges is remarkably high — around 60 percent — precisely because the prior reviews within the Social Security bureaucracy are totally independent of each other and, therefore, prone to minor inconsistencies of the sort which some judges are delighted to use to reverse the Administration. The Grace Commission described this travesty of justice: "What is happening is that internal S.S.A. appeals are serving more to create legally reversible decisions as opposed to reviewing the merits and facts of particular cases. Hence, many people who, according to the facts of the case, do not deserve benefits, end up getting them because of the ineffective appeals process." The Commission concludes that a "uniform appeals system within S.S.A. would go a long way to fix the situation and, in so doing, would save taxpayers $3.6 billion over three years." And that, fellow taxpayer, is *double* the amount paid in federal individual income and employment taxes by the residents of Nevada in 1982.

The Social Security bureaucracy has produced a manual called the *Program Operations Manual System,* which it sends to those who process claims within the Administration. The Grace Commission comments: "The manual is large; if its 45,000 recipients stacked their copies atop one another, the pile would be 34 miles high — equivalent to 139 Empire State Buildings." Not only that, but "each recipient *also* receives 12,000 pages of annual P.O.M.S. revisions each year. Social Security Administration

(S.S.A.) 'allows' each recipient one hour per week for reviewing and filing, which means each recipient would have to read, understand and file one page of revisions every 16 seconds of time allowed to avoid breaking the rules.'' And what is the cost to the taxpayer? The Commission continues: ''Assuming 45,000 recipients actually spend one hour a week each on this exercise…that annual cost for this paper-shuffling is $25 million,'' and perhaps even ''a multiple of that figure.''

Another vexing problem confronting Social Security — and hurting taxpayers — is the growing abuse of the system by foreign citizens living in other countries. These are aliens who have worked in the U.S. and contributed to Social Security while here, then left the country. When Social Security benefits began in 1940, the Commission reports, ''there were only 100 beneficiaries abroad who received $12,000. For 1981, these numbers had grown to 313,000 and nearly $1 billion.'' Of that number, an estimated 206,100 (66 percent) were aliens, most of them alien dependents. ''The average alien family,'' the Commission continues, ''has received about $30,000 since 1961, which is about $24 in benefits for every $1 in FICA taxes paid before retirement.''

The food stamp program is a major source of transfer-payment fraud and abuse. ''Most of the loss,'' the Commission notes, ''is due to households that obtain more Food Stamp benefits than they should or the receipt of benefits by completely ineligible households.'' The Commission charges that too many recipients have their reported income accepted at face value without additional verification. Without such verification, the temptation is to falsify income declarations — and it happens too frequently.

There are other problems with the food stamp program

which contribute to the wasteful expenditure of tax dollars. The Grace Commission notes, for instance, that Food Stamps are provided "to certain members of the military who qualify because the cost of government-furnished housing is not included in their pay for the purpose of determining food stamp benefits." Also, the Commission continues, "if a member of the armed forces is assigned away from his home for an extended tour of duty, a common occurence in all of the Services, he or she is, according to food stamp guidelines, 'no longer a member of the household.' The total income earned is not counted — only the money sent home through pay 'allotments.'" The result is that many military families are supplementing their household incomes with food stamps which they do not actually need.

The present Thrifty Food Plan (T.F.P.) used to compute food stamp benefits is seriously outdated. It is based, for instance, on the average household in 1971, which consisted of two adults and two children. Today's average family, on the other hand, consists of an average of 2.6 persons with higher percentages of both women and children. Relying on the outdated formula results in benefits significantly greater than stated requirements. Updating it would result in savings of $3.4 billion over three years; that's what the combined residents of Vermont, Montana, Wyoming, Maine, and North Dakota paid in federal individual income tax in 1981.

The use of food stamps rather than cash was intended to assure that the benefits were indeed used for food. The Commission reports, however, that such is not always the case "as food coupons are used to buy a multitude of non-food items, such as houses or cars." Also, the program has generated large-scale (and enormously costly) fraud and abuse. The investigation of food-stamp abuses (especially fraud and "trafficking" in stolen or otherwise illegally-obtained stamps, usually at a discounted price) devours *one-fourth* of the Agriculture Department Inspector General's yearly budget.

The Commission also reports that the food-stamp fraud continues even after the stamps are used by the recipients. "A number of grocery stores," for instance, "make out quite well by accepting food stamps and, in accordance with regulations, issuing store credit slips, rather than cash, for change of less than 50 cents. Many of these credit slips are never used, but the stores are reimbursed for the full value of the original food stamps." An investigation of the situation by the Inspector General's office resulted in an estimate that this practice has lined the pockets of grocery store operators with at least $30 million in food-stamp dollars.

CHAPTER SIX
Postal Service

There are currently some 40,000 postal units around the nation including 30,242 post offices and 9,215 stations, branches, and community post offices. In 1964 and 1967, the General Accounting Office (G.A.O.) concluded that U.S. Postal Service costs could be cut significantly by closing small post offices. Mail service would be continued by extending rural routes and establishing contractor-operated post offices. In 1975, another G.A.O. report found that 12,000 small post offices could be closed — without a decline in the quality of service — for an estimated annual savings of $100 million. But the mere thought of closing post offices sparked such sharp reaction, particularly in the postal union, that Congress passed legislation limiting the Postal Service's authority to close the facilities.

In September of 1982, the G.A.O. issued yet another report on the issue. It again found substantial potential for savings (between $125 million and $150 million annually by 1990) if 7,000 limited-use mail service post offices were replaced with alternative services acceptable to the public, such as rural route extensions and community post offices. The G.A.O. discovered from a survey of postal patrons whose post offices had already been replaced that some 88 percent were satisfied with their current service. But bureaucratic resistance works in ingenious ways. As the Grace Commission wryly observed: "At the rate the Postal Service is following up on the G.A.O.'s recommendations, they should have all consolidation accomplished by the year 2087 . . . "

The Commission recommends (1) that Congress eliminate the current legislative barriers to replacement so that the Postal Service may "realize more quickly the savings associated with replacement actions," and (2) that the Postal Service streamline service to rural areas "by replac-

28

ing limited mail service offices with alternative services which are publicly acceptable." The potential three-year savings: $272 million.

. **Contract Stations** *(Potential Savings: $165.6 million over three years).* One of the alternatives for replacement of limited mail service post offices is the contract station operated by the private sector. Based on contracts negotiated with the Postal Service, such stations are, in the words of the Grace Commission, "permitted to operate with flexible hours . . . in areas of high visibility and convenience to large numbers of postal customers." The stations "operate with a retailer providing space in an existing store or office. The retailer must be bonded and submit selected employees for postal training and orientation. In exchange for negotiated annual fees, U.S.P.S. provides stamp stock and other products and materials necessary to conduct retail and, in some cases, delivery transactions (postal boxes)." The Postal Service itself estimates that the costs for contract stations range from 2.8 cents to 12 cents per dollar of earned revenue. In contrast, regular retail postal windows at Postal Service facilities may cost as much as 24 cents per revenue dollar. (Self-service postal centers operate at 8 cents to 10 cents.) Private sector mail delivery companies, such as Federal Express, have already shown that free enterprise can outperform the U.S.P.S. — at lower cost. Privatizing at least some part of the current system would almost certainly improve service to customers.

The Grace Commission recommends that the Postal Service "aggressively market and pursue the addition of contract stations . . . in all areas where efficiencies may be gained." The potential three-year savings to taxpayers: $165.6 million.

Checks and Balances *(Potential Savings: $60 million*

over three years). Another potential savings area involves the 22.4 million checks which the Postal Service issues annually. The Grace Commission reported that the "Treasury Department in effect provides the checking account at an average cost of $1.01 per check." Yet, with such a massive volume of checks, the Postal Service "could easily substitute commercial-bank checking services, which would probably charge $.10 per check or one-tenth the Treasury's cost." Even if the private-sector charge were $.20 per check, the service "could save $60 million in three years just . . . issuing checks."

Update Mailing Lists *(Potential Savings: $96 million over three years).* The Government Printing Office currently distributes publications without charge, costing taxpayers about $535 million each year. Part of that cost is the result of waste, the printing of unnecessary copies — and out-dated mailing lists. The Grace Commission recommends that a greater effort be made to update the lists, and that they be centralized, where appropriate, to avoid duplication. The savings to taxpayers would likely reach $96 million over three years.

Sick Leave *(Potential Savings: $135 million over three years).* During Fiscal Year 1981, Postal Service employees averaged 8.8 sick days each, which is 60 percent more than the 5.5 day average for the private sector. The cost to taxpayers of those 21,734 lost work-*years* was $652 million. If only 1/16th of that loss (*i.e.*, one-half day per worker) could be recovered, the savings would be $135 million over three years.

Non-delivery of Correctly-Addressed Mail *(Potential Savings: $30.4 million over three years).* An unusually serious and costly Postal Service problem is the sizable percentage of correctly addressed, third-class bulk advertising mail that is never delivered. Once such mail is deemed to be "U.A.A." (Undeliverable As Addressed), and to have "no obvious value," postal regulations authorize its destruction unless it is specifically endorsed "Forwarding and Return Postage Guaranteed" or something equivalent. In the case of third-class business mail, there is no way for the sender to know that his advertising message failed to reach its intended source.

Mailers have been suspicious for years that a certain percentage of properly addressed mail was being treated as U.A.A. mail and not being delivered by the Postal Service. Until 1981, little comprehensive and statistically valid data were available. But in September and October of that year, one major book company conducted a test to determine whether all properly addressed mail (including bulk third-class advertising mail) was delivered. The test revealed that a shocking 8.4 percent of typical advertising pieces, properly mailed and addressed, were *not* delivered, while 6.6 percent of pieces endorsed "Forwarding and Return Postage Guaranteed" were not delivered.

In 1980 and 1981, the Postal Service conducted its own Diagnostic Survey Analysis Testing program to measure delivery time. In both the private-sector and Postal Service studies, the special mailing lists used were verified for accuracy prior to mailing. But the analysis also revealed that 5 - 44 percent of third-class mail, and 3 - 18 percent of second-class mail was "not received".

It is important to note that such non-delivery of accurately addressed mail hurts not only the private-sector firm doing the mailing, but the Postal Service as well. For instance, so-called "nonpreferential" mail (especially third class) is a significant growth segment of today's Postal Service. As the Grace Commission observed: "Any problems

31

in delivery performance could have a detrimental effect on this important market segment. Problems such as nondelivery of third class advertising mail could cause mailers to consider switching to other forms of advertising. Thus, U.S.P.S. faces the risk of losing the growth segment of its market, unless these mailers are given acceptable service performance." Another crucial consideration, so far as the Postal Service itself is concerned, is the impact of the non-delivery problem on other classes of mail. A significant percentage of third-class mail is advertising that can generate additional volume for the Postal Service. The Grace Commission comments: "Based on a study, one major mailer estimated that one respondent to a third class advertising piece can generate as many as 43 additional pieces of first, third, and fourth class mail within a year. Other major mailers contacted estimated that additional pieces generated could easily exceed 43 pieces; e.g., a response accepting a subscription to a weekly magazine."

Applying an average of eight percent non-delivered to the 24.7 billion pieces of regular third-class bulk rate mail indicates the magnitude of the problem. The Grace Commission reports: "Using conservative estimates of additional volume generated by respondents to third class mail, and assuming a response rate of 1 percent if this mail were delivered, leads to an estimate of up to 652 million pieces of mail that could be generated."

The Commission recommends that the Postal Service take the necessary steps to "reduce the estimated 8 percent of properly mailed and addressed nondelivered third class mail to 4 percent." Doing so would result in savings of $30.4 million over three years. And that doesn't even include the incalculable *indirect* revenue impact resulting from the factors mentioned above.

CHAPTER SEVEN
Collecting Debts

As of June 30, 1982, about 16 percent of the total $219 billion in receivables due the government were delinquent. How did this happen? The Grace Commission found that the government, as a result of lax and inefficient debt collection strategy, is permitting literally *billions* of dollars to be written off. With a little ingenuity and added effort, much of that tax money could be recovered.

The following examples cited by the Commission confirm that a great number of federal debt delinquencies are indeed unwarranted, since many delinquent borrowers have *not* fallen on hard times through illness, indigency, or other misfortunes.

(1) In 1982, the General Accounting Office (G.A.O.) did a report on delinquent student loans made to people who are now health care and nursing professionals. The study concluded that many of the borrowers had the means to repay. In reviewing delinquent accounts, it was found that 72 percent of the borrowers were current on private-sector debts, and 67 percent had been extended private-sector credit exceeding the amount of their debts to the taxpayer. For example, one health professional, delinquent for more than *three years* in repaying a student-loan balance of $2,940, had somehow managed to pay off two commercial loans for $13,200, was current on a $56,000 loan to purchase real estate, and had credit lines totalling $7,700 with several banks and department stores!

(2) A 1981 G.A.O. study reported that a sample of veterans who were delinquent in reimbursing educational assistance overpayments included 56 percent who had good credit ratings; 57 percent who had been extended credit by the private sector that exceeded the amount of their outstanding debts to the V.A.; and 81 percent who were employed, including 6 percent with the federal govern-

ment. In fact, two of these were actually working for the V.A. The study also described an instance where the government stopped trying to collect an overpayment from one veteran after "determining" that he had insufficient income to make legal action worthwhile. Subsequently, a credit bureau report revealed that the debtor was employed and had obtained an unsecured bank loan for $1,100 only nine months after the government's collection efforts ended.

(3) A report by the Department of Education's Inspector General reveals that, as recently as 1982, there were 46,860 current and retired federal employees who had defaulted on student loans. Total value of those loans: $68 million.

In the words of the Grace Commission, "high delinquencies as a result of weak collection efforts not only make for inequalities among borrowers, but they ultimately reduce funds that could be available to other potential beneficiaries."

Some 95 percent of the total debt owed to the government is managed by 24 different agencies, each of which has its own way of doing things. The resulting lack of uniformity impedes both the tracking and collection of debts. Since any debt collections that are made are turned into the Treasury, it does not benefit an agency to spend time or effort in such collections. The Grace Commission suggests that more-uniform methods and definitions of terms be used in the debt collection process, combined with the establishment of incentives for agencies to collect their debts (such as letting them retain a portion of the collections). The Commission believes that such measures could result in a $9.3 billion reduction in the federal deficit over three years.

The Department of Justice serves as a collections attorney for other federal agencies and also acts as attorney n behalf of the United States in cases dealing with the collection of civil and criminal fines and claims owed to the nited States. The Grace Commission tried to discover ays that the Justice Department could, by making certain olicy adjustments, collect and manage outstanding debt ceivables more efficiently than it is at present.

For instance, a lack of uniformity in the claims which riginate in other agencies, and are referred to the Department of Justice, is a major hindrance to effective debt collection. Currently, each agency establishes credit policies d procedures (and even uses its own definitions for key rms) to serve its particular purposes. As the Commission otes, the Justice Department "encounters serious difficulties attempting to deal consistently with referrals of arying status." The Commission therefore recommends at the Department require a uniform reporting system for aims it receives from other agencies. Also, a special assistnt U.S. attorney in charge of debt collection should be amed to work with other agencies to facilitate cooperation assuring oversight of all aspects of the debt collection ocess. The Commission further urges the use of private ollection agencies, so far as is practical, to aid in the collection of debts. If we were to implement these recommendtions, the Commission claims, you, the taxpayer, would ve $5 million in interest, $44.2 million in "cash acceleraons," and $626.1 million in additional revenues. That lds up to $675.3 million, an amount equal to the federal come and Social Security taxes paid by 163,345 mediancome families in 1983.

The Department of Housing and Urban Development I.U.D.) collects debts from approximately 50 programs. ne of those is the Section 8 housing program, the largest six H.U.D. housing programs. Section 8 had estimated

outlays of $3.9 billion in Fiscal Year 1982. Under Secti
8, H.U.D. makes up the difference between what a lo
income household can afford and what the free market se
as rent for an adequate housing unit. The Inspector Gener
has *conservatively* estimated, according to the Grace Co
mission, "that *between 12 and 17 percent of the tenar
receiving housing subsidies under the Section 8 progra
falsify information to gain benefits.*" One reason w
falsifiers get away with this involves a handbook produc
by H.U.D. The book is supposed "to determine applica
eligibility in accordance with federal regulations, but t
requirement for verification is very general in nature an
does not stress the need to establish the applicant's incom
As a result, each of the local housing authorities are inte
preting the H.U.D. handbooks individually and each h
different methods to obtain the required information."

As of September 30, 1981, $1.6 billion of the $13
billion accounts and loans receivable (11.8 percent) we
delinquent. In reviewing H.U.D. procedures, the Gra
Commission learned that the department makes only thr
attempts each year to collect charged-off (closed-out) a
counts. The private sector makes between 24 and 36 su
attempts annually. The department's success rate is
anemic 15 to 20 percent; the private sector collects 80 to
percent. Rather than simply forwarding charged-off a
counts to headquarters to lay dormant, the Grace Commi
sion recommends that such accounts be assigned to privat
sector collection agencies. Consider the possibilities:

Between 1975 and 1981, the dollar amount of charge
off H.U.D. accounts (those the agency has stopped tryir
to collect) totaled $92,014,000. Let us suppose, as does t
Grace Commission, that $27,604,000, or 30 percent,
that amount is truly uncollectible. That would leave

potentially collectible amount of $64,410,000. Next, let us assume that one-half of that amount ($32,205,000) also turns out to be irretrievable, even for our private-sector collection agency. That would drop the total to the amount the agency *was* able to collect: $32,205,000. Finally, subtract from that amount the usual 40 percent agency collection fee ($12,882,000), and the remaining $19,323,000 represents the likely net recovery to H.U.D. from those "lost" accounts. That figure equals the federal income taxes paid by 8,566 median-income American families in 1983. Indeed, the Grace Commission thinks the government could save $1.8 billion, in the first year alone, by using collection agencies and credit bureaus to supplement the debt collection efforts of government agencies.

The Public Health Service (P.H.S.) student-loan program is aimed at increasing the number of health professionals in the country in general, and the number of such professionals eligible for service in Health Manpower Shortage Areas in particular. The total program has outlays of $930 million, of which $45 million (4.8 percent) is considered delinquent. The targeted delinquency rate is one-tenth of the loans total, or $4.6 million. A problem in lowering the delinquency rate, however, is that the P.H.S. charges only $1 as a late payment for the first month, then $2 for each subsequent month. And the minimum monthly payment required is only $15, which does not even cover processing costs. Such "penalties" hardly create an incentive to repay loans promptly. The Grace Commission recommends taking whatever legislative and/or administrative steps might be necessary to make possible a meaningful increase in the penalties applied to delinquent loans.

Some $124 million in first-year debt collections could be brought in if the Veterans Administration used such private-sector practices as credit-bureau reporting telephone calls, and small-claims court in collecting loans These savings would reach $208 million over three years accompanied by a $12 million reduction in interest due on the National Debt.

For the years 1979-1981, the Small Business Administration had from 4.2 to 5.2 times the number of uncollectible loans as did the private sector. The Grace Commission found that S.B.A. loans "that have been charged off are not currently worked for further collection." As with H.U.D. the S.B.A. simply gives up before the fight is over Needless to say, the Commission recommended the use of private collection services. Beginning with Fiscal Year 1978 through May 31, 1982, net S.B.A. charge-offs of supposedly uncollectible debts totalled $844.1 million. "If these charge-offs were worked by competent professionals," the Commission asserts, "a recovery of at least 10 percent should be realized." We think 10 percent is very conservative. But even assuming that low figure, over three years, total revenues of $118.5 million could be realized. That equals the federal income and Social Security taxes paid by 30,785 median-income families in 1983.

The default rate on direct and federally-insured student loans is 16 percent, while the rate for guaranteed student loans is 9 percent. A total of $2.2 billion in student loans is in default, some of it for more than ten years. The Grace Commission contends that if "standard private sector collection policies and procedures were used to cut the default rate to the typical private sector level of 3 percent, $497 million could be saved over three years."

Part of the problem in collecting student loans is that the government maintains three separate and distinct student loan programs: (a) Federally Insured Student Loan

38

(F.I.S.L.), which are made by banks and insured by the federal government; (b) National Direct Student Loans (N.D.S.L.), which are made and insured by the government through local educational institutions; and (c) Guaranteed Student Loans (G.S.L.), which are made by banks, but insured by state agencies and reinsured by the federal government. The Grace Commission asserts that keeping the three programs separate "makes administration difficult, causes duplication and increases waste, fraud, abuse and error." Similar benefits, it contends, "could be provided to students by . . . consolidating the three programs into one." Specifically, the Commission urges that the N.D.S.L. programs be consolidated into "the more cost-effective G.S.L. program," a move which "would return at least $290 million per year, or $870 million over three years, to the Treasury until the approximately $5 billion now outstanding in N.D.S.L. loans and advances to institutions for new loans has been fully recovered." The Commission notes that, additionally, "$185.9 million in interest savings over three years will result" from the consolidation. That's equal to the federal income taxes paid by 8,381 median-income families in 1983.

We have mentioned only a few of the federal agencies and programs which have been plagued with deadbeats. It now remains to be seen if Congress, the president, and the agencies themselves, will unite to implement the many positive recommendations tendered by the Grace Commission to solve, or at least control, this expensive and frustrating problem. Those who borrow money should pay it back; they should not be allowed to hold innocent taxpayers as hostages to their personal debts. But *you* must let Congress and the president know that you care about making your government collect debts from these deadbeats.

CHAPTER EIGHT
Cash Management

A good deal of waste results from inefficient financial management by the federal government: The Grace Commission discovered, for instance, deficiencies in the handling of cash resources that cost the government surprising amounts each day. The Commission found the government could reap three-year savings of $9 billion in additional interest, just by collecting and depositing funds more quickly than it does now. The Interior Department's cash management system, for one, was found to be so inadequate that it often takes more than two weeks to collect, record and deposit savings. The cost to taxpayers? Between $23.2 million and $58.8 million in lost interest over three years. A somewhat similar situation was discovered during the Commission's scrutiny of Navy policy. A substantial amount of cash (perhaps $5 billion annually) is received and deposited by Navy Finance Centers. Often, the funds are not deposited on the day received, but are instead held until the required accounting can be completed, which can take several days. Assuming that the Navy's receipts were to be deposited only two days earlier than they now are, the annual savings (interest earned) would be $3.6 million.

Waiting to pay bills until they are actually due is an even more important procedure. The government could save $6.3 billion just by keeping its funds in interest-bearing accounts as long as possible. Even the time schedules for postal pick-ups are crucial, the Commission explains, declaring that they should be "carefully monitored so that checks sent through the mail arrive on the last day they are due, not earlier." If a check due on Monday arrives instead on the previous Thursday, for instance, the government loses the interest that could have accrued over the weekend.

On one occasion, nine recipients of grants from the Department of Transportation paid contractors $473 million in bills an average of 13 days before they were actually due. According to the Grace Commission, "the needless interest expense incurred cost taxpayers $2.9 million."

So the timely payment of bills is indeed significant. The Commission asserts that, "if the federal government stopped paying bills early, it would reduce cash outlays by $6.3 billion in the first year of implementation . . . . Promptly paying the bills it now pays late would, however, offset about $1.4 billion of this benefit. Nevertheless, the *net result of paying all* bills when due is $4.9 billion in additional cash in the government's *bank accounts* — or, alternatively, a $4.9 billion reduction in the amount of money the government needs to borrow to cover deficits." That being the case, the government will not have to pay interest on $4.9 billion it otherwise would have to borrow — resulting in a first-year savings (assuming 10 percent interest) of $490 million. And, the Commission continues: "The second year, the base interest savings is again $490 million, but there is also an additional $49 million interest savings because the federal government would not have to borrow the $490 million to pay the first year's interest." Carrying on through the third year, the calculations add up to a total three-year savings in interest of $1.6 *billion*! All from simply paying bills exactly when they are due.

Treasury Financial Communications System *(Potential Savings: $194 million over three years).* The T.F.C.S. is an on-line electronic access to the country's banking system. During Fiscal Year 1982, it processed nearly $200 billion in wire transfers and can presently handle 10,000 messages each day. The current average minimum transaction on the system is $50,000 (any amount less than that is usually handled by the Postal Service, which takes an average of two to four days to complete the transfer, leaving the dollars "idle" during a time when they could be earning interest). The Grace Commission recommends lowering the T.F.C.S. minimum to $10,000. The system can handle it and the accelerated cash flow could save taxpayers $194 million in interest over three years.

Paychecks *(Potential Savings: $130 million a year).* It costs the government about 26.5 cents to process a paycheck; it is only about four cents if the transaction is done by electronic transfer. Multiply the difference of 22.5 cents by the approximate 74.3 million federal salary payments each year, and another 510 million recurring benefit payments. The total potential cost reduction, just for processing paychecks, is more than $130 million a year! And that is what 33,916 median-income families paid in federal income and Social Security taxes for 1983.

Criminal Cash *(Potential Savings: $49.8 million over three years).* During its investigations, and when making arrests, the Justice Department seizes sizable amounts of property (including money) from suspects. Currently, the confiscated money is held by the Department until the case is adjudicated. Why not, the Grace Commission asks, deposit that money in the U.S. Treasury while awaiting the outcome of the legal proceedings? Doing so would be perfectly legal and would generate an estimated $49.8 million in additional interest over three years.

* * *

The Commission notes that "other management tools such as electronic fund transfers, automatic account withdrawal and controlling advances by letters of credit for checks paid would conserve cash resources and save interest.'' So would stopping advance Defense Department payments to contractors, a move which by itself would generate three-year savings and cash acceleration of $17.9 million.

If all of its recommendations for cash management are fully implemented, the Commission estimates that ''a one-time reduction in cash needs of $21 billion is achievable, based on the federal government's daily cash flow of $7 billion and assuming a three-day reduction in cash needs during the first year of implementation. This would result in a $21 billion reduction in the national debt, which in turn would lead to interest savings of $2.1 billion the first year (at a 10 percent interest rate) and $7.0 billion over three years.'' Consider that the $2.1 billion is equal to the federal income taxes paid by 897,435 median-income families in 1983!

CHAPTER NINE
Agriculture

The Department of Agriculture (U.S.D.A.) helps farmers by providing research, credit, insurance, price supports, production and market information, and marketing assistance. The Department also assists consumers with nutritional information, regulations on safety and health, and food for low-income persons. The Grace Commission ran across a number of Department-related activities which are needlessly squandering tax dollars. Here are some examples:

Farmers Home Administration Loans *(Potential Savings: $2.3 billion over three years)*. A full 70 percent of those who borrow money from the Farmer's Home Administration (Fm.H.A.) are not farmers. The delinquency rate among non-farm borrowers is 26 percent, more than *seven times* the private-sector average of three to four percent. The expertise of Fm.H.A. is supposedly in the area of farming, yet a sizable portion of its current activity involves housing, business, and community-development loans. The Grace Commission recommends that such non-farm loans be transferred to more appropriate agencies such as the Department of Housing and Urban Development and the Small Business Administration. Any farm loans handled by those agencies should be transferred to Fm.H.A. Such realignment of loan type with lending expertise, the Commission asserts, "should permit Fm.H.A. to reduce the current 43 percent delinquency rate on farm loans and save about $34 million in the first year." And, another $135 million could be saved through such steps as phasing out Fm.H.A.'s *direct* loan program while continuing its *guaranteed* loan program at a reduced level of 75 percent (rather than the present 90 percent). Dropping the guarantee level would go far to encourage improved loan performance by private-sector lenders.

Incorporating these and other Commission proposals for streamlining its operations could enhance Fm.H.A.'s financial picture by $2.3 billion in cost savings, new revenues, and cash acceleration over three years. This is the same amount that all the taxpayers of Arkansas paid in federal individual income and employment taxes in 1982.

Agricultural Cooperative Service *(Potential Savings: $4.9 million over three years).* The Commission recommended that the A.C.S. recover the costs of its research and educational publications through an appropriate user fee. By charging for its literature and the technical assistance services it renders to cooperatives, the A.C.S. could realize enhanced revenues of $4.9 million in three years.

Foreign Agricultural Service *(Potential Savings: $24.5 million over four years).* Since the early 1960's, the F.A.S. has provided direct funding to a number of market development organizations which develop and maintain foreign markets for certain U.S.-produced commodities. The Grace Commission concluded that it is inappropriate for the government to continue the open-ended funding of such organizations and that the F.A.S. program should be phased out gradually, but *entirely,* over a four-year period. "If cooperator groups are useful market development tools," the Commission asserted, "their projects should more properly be funded by the private sector . . . . If their members are not willing to finance them, it is not the Government's responsibility to intervene." The savings to taxpayers would total $24.5 million by the end of the four-year phase-out period.

Consolidation *(Potential Savings: $22 million over three years).* The Commission discovered that three Agriculture Department agencies perform duplicative research analysis. Consolidation of "the Economic

Research Service, the Foreign Agricultural Service, and the World Agricultural Outlook Board into a single entity, and elimination of the overlap in functions, could save $22 million over three years.''

Agricultural Research Service. The Grace Commission also expressed concern regarding the continuing expansion of the A.R.S. The fact is that the 148 already-existing A.R.S. domestic centers are seriously under-utilized. In October of 1981, the A.R.S. ''was using its laboratory space at only 73 percent of capacity, and in some cases at a rate as low as 17 percent of capacity.'' Yet, in 1979 Congress had appropriated $33.7 million to construct three new facilities, and another $1.5 million to plan two others. When operational, the expense of some 500 additional scientists and support personnel will also have to be added to the equation. The Commission agrees that ''[m]odern facilities are needed for meaningful research,'' but warns that ''unless A.R.S. closes some older units, its already poor utilization rate will deteriorate further while its costs continue to rise.''

Postmortem Poultry Inspection *(Potential Savings: $307.8 million).* Department of Agriculture inspectors are currently required to oversee the slaughter of poultry and the processing of poultry products shipped interstate or to foreign markets. The purpose is to assure a poultry supply which is wholesome, as well as properly marked, labeled, and packaged. The Grace Commission recommends that, where the Department determines that inspection activities by plant employees would be equivalent in quality and effectiveness to those of government personnel, such inspections be conducted by plant employees. And where the Department does not make such a determination, and its own inspectors must continue to perform the service, user charges should be assessed to recover the full cost of the inspections. By either privatizing the inspections, or recovering their cost through user fees collected from the poultry plants, the savings to taxpayers over three years would total $307.8 million.

Wool Incentives *(Potential Savings: in the millions).* The federal government spends millions each year on a program to encourage domestic wool production. The program was launched in 1954, when wool was considered to be an essential and strategic commodity for U.S. commercial and military items. But since that time, the increased use of synthetic fibers and imported wool has greatly reduced the demand for domestic wool. Nevertheless, in 1980 the government spent $42.1 million on the program, thereby helping to increase wool output by between seven and 16 million pounds. As the Grace Commission notes, "each additional pound — whose market value was about $.88 — cost the Government between $2.63 and $6.01" — hardly a cost-effective expenditure of tax dollars.

CHAPTER TEN
Controlling Health Care Spending

Total U.S. health-care expenditures swelled from $41.7 billion in 1965 to $322.4 billion in 1982, an average increase of 12.8 percent per year. Federal health care expenditures, by comparison, started from a base of $5.5 billion in 1965 and soared to $93.1 billion by 1982, for an average annual increase of 18.1 percent.

Those percentages are consistent with others documenting the profligacy of government compared to — well, compared to just about anything else. Private-sector health plans, for example, cost an average of $93 per month, per family. That is a full third less than the federal health plan average of $139 per family. As a percentage of payroll, the average is 5.8 percent for the private sector versus 6.8 percent for the government. And while a difference of only one percent might not seem large, it slapped an additional $618 million burden on taxpayers in 1981. The Grace Commission asserts that bringing "the average in line with private sector experience would save taxpayers $1.4 billion over three years" — the same amount paid in federal income and Social Security taxes by 3,652 median-income families in 1983.

Federal workers are allowed to accumulate sick leave without limit, then add any unused days onto total service in calculating retirement annuities. This is practically unheard of in the private sector. Ending it would save taxpayers $1.1 billion over three years.

In 1980, 6.3 percent of federal employees filed on-the-job injury claims. Slightly more than half of that number (3.2 percent) lost time from work. In contrast, the Metropolitan Life Insurance Company reported that only 1.7 percent of private-sector employees filed injury claims, with one-quarter (.42 percent) losing time from work.

Many individuals who are eligible for medical care at

military hospitals also carry private health insurance. Historically, however, the Defense Department has made little attempt to collect the cost of caring for such beneficiaries from their private insurance carriers. By implementing a program vigorously to pursue reimbursement from private carriers, the Grace Commission believes that at least $1.2 billion in new revenue could be realized over three years.

Federal hospitals acquire their medical supplies from several sources: (a) federally-operated supply depots; (b) purchase orders against nationally-negotiated, indefinite-quantity contracts; (c) open-market purchases negotiated at the local level; and (d) orders placed on the open market without negotiations. Of the four possibilities, local-level purchasing is the most widely used and accounts for 40 percent of all federal purchases. In contrast, the private sector purchases from 75 to 85 percent of its medical supplies through more cost-efficient national contracts. Bringing federal policy more in line with the private sector approach could effect three-year savings of $221.8 million.

It is a stipulation of the Medicare program that reimbursements to hospitals for the goods and services they procure from outside suppliers are not to be used to provide a profit to such suppliers. The Grace Commission learned, however, that "hospitals which procure goods and services from organizations related to them by common ownership or control often circumvent the law and provide the supplier with a profit because the reimbursement process is difficult to audit." In one instance cited by the Commission, a "Las Vegas hospital was able to reimburse a related pharmacy for intravenous solution costing 800 percent more than it should, resulting in $215,000 in Medicare/Medicaid overpayments over two years." In another instance, a "California hospital was able to lease equipment from a related organization for eight years at rates $500,000 above cost." And yet another California hospital "was able to grant itself the equivalent of an interest-free $500,000 loan."

The pacemakers which hospitals purchase for Medicare patients cost an average of $3,424, which is some 21 percent more than the $2,833 price for identical models listed on the General Service Administration's Federal Supply Schedule (F.S.S.). The Grace Commission recommends that pacemaker prices be brought in line with F.S.S. rates to save the Medicare program $64 million annually. That is the same amount paid in Social Security taxes by 39,628 median-income families in 1983.

Since the expense of surgery is covered by Medicaid and Medicare, beneficiaries often submit to recommended surgery without bothering to determine if it is actually needed. The Grace Commission recommends that a second medical opinion be required for elective surgeries, and that such a requirement could reduce the cost of such surgeries by as much as 29 percent for Medicaid and 18 percent for Medicare. That would translate into annual savings of $158 million, an amount equivalent to the federal income and Social Security taxes paid by 3,833 medium-income families in 1983.

In 1972, the Defense Department established the Uniform Services University of the Health Sciences (U.S.U.H.S.) to train medical students to become military doctors. According to the Grace Commission: "It costs $77,186 per year to train a student at U.S.U.H.S. as of F.Y. [*Fiscal Year*] 1983 versus $19,146 through the Health Professions Scholarship Program, the primary source of physicians for the military." There is simply no convincing evidence, the Commission contends, "that further opera-

ion of U.S.U.H.S. is justified, and closing the facility
would save taxpayers $115 million in three years.''

The Health Care Financing Administration (H.C.F.A.)
reimburses hospitals for Medicare expenses. The hospitals
determine the fees and bill the government. The Grace
Commission suggests that a "major incentive to control
costs could be achieved by H.C.F.A.'s determining
scheduled fees in advance'' since "the hospitals' prof-
itability would be increased or decreased by how well *they*
stayed within the guidelines.'' Six states are now using this
method; if implemented nationwide it could save $5.7
billion in excess charges over three years.

The Grace Commission outlines a fascinating plan for
bringing federal health spending under control by placing a
cap on total spending, and by bringing competition into the
picture through a fair and sensible system of bidding.

The first step would be to establish a fiscally acceptable
limitation on total federal health-care expenditures. The
Commission recommends setting this fiscal guideline so
that federal expenditures on all health-care programs "are
restricted to increases no faster than the overall rate of
growth in the U.S. economy, i.e., by approximately 8-10
percent per year.''

Step two would establish *per capita* spending limits, accompanied by protection against any reductions. For Fiscal
Year 1984, for instance, the program goals would be met
with "average federal expenditures of no more than $2,140
per Medicare beneficiary and $1,000 per Medicaid
beneficiary, excluding the state/local portion and $1,900
per Medicaid beneficiary including the state/local
portion.''

Step three would be geographic allocations, based on the
number of persons served by Medicare and Medicaid in

each region. The geographic areas would be as large a possible.

Step four would be competitive bidding. Based on the *pe capita* spending rates for each program, the governmer would invite competitive bids from the private sector an state and local health-care systems to provide services t beneficiaries. Appropriate steps would be taken to assur that Medicare and Medicaid services still would not co either government or beneficiaries any more than contrac tually agreed expenditure levels.

In return for assuming the risks involved in the commin ment to provide coverage, the successful bidders woul have the chance to earn profits (or sustain losses) based o how well they meet the cost targets underlying their con petitive bids. Thus, an incentive would be introduced int the system to cut waste and increase efficiency.

Also, consumers would "retain the flexibility of seekin their own health care providers on an illness-by-illnes basis." Indeed, recipients would be given vouchers " purchase their own insurance or join group health plans. Hospitals, doctors and other providers with acceptable bid would serve the Medicare and Medicaid populations, bu enrollees would be free to choose among these participatin providers. That would establish more incentives on the pa of hospitals and doctors to provide better service to patient — at lower costs.

The fifth and final step of the Grace Commission pla would assure consumer choice. "Bidders would be free,' the Commission stresses, "to submit plans with premiu costs which are more than the maximum *per capita* amour which the federal government will finance. Consumer would be free to choose these more costly plans, provide they pay the excess of premium costs over the governmer allowance." There would be periodic enrollment periods when enrollees would be given an opportunity to change their form of coverage. "The freedom of enrollees to select and change their own coverage," the Commission asserts, "is an essential factor in making competitive markets work. Plans must be subject to the risk of failure in the marketplace, if costs are to be contained." Also, the Commission continues, "possible rejection by enrollees is the best assurance of satisfactory quality and responsive service, though the federal government would retain responsibility for insuring that coverage is at least comparable to what would have been offered by the Medicare and Medicaid programs."

* * *

That, in a nutshell, is the Grace Commission's proposal for improving our nation's health-care system. And the projected three-year savings is estimated to be $28.9 billion — an amount equal to the federal income taxes paid in 1981 by the individual taxpayers of Alaska, Arizona, Arkansas, Delaware, District of Columbia, Hawaii, Idaho, Maine, Mississippi, Montana, Nebraska, Nevada, New Hampshire, North Carolina, Oregon, Rhode Island, South Carolina, South Dakota, Utah, Vermont, West Virginia and Wyoming.

CHAPTER ELEVEN
Construction

The federal government currently engages in virtually every sort of construction project under authority granted to 26 separate agencies. The Grace Commission concluded: "Federal construction projects are characterized by mismanagement and confusion at all stages of the construction process." Indeed, the Commission estimated that contracting out construction activities to the private sector would probably result in three-year savings of $143 million.

Whereas private-sector engineering and construction firms traditionally appoint a project manager for each major project or group of small projects, federal agencies typically do not. And much of the increased cost of federal construction projects may result from the lack of a single individual with a mandate to plan, organize, staff, direct, control, and lead each project. With so many cooks attending the broth, the average project takes seven years from planning to completion, and even then, only 24 months are spent on actual construction. The other five years are consumed by delays, redundant revisions, etc. According to the Grace Commission: "Virtually all project completions are delayed at least 12 months, costing about $50 million in waste annually. Adopting a project manager approach would save $166 million over three years."

One problem, the Grace Commission found, is that there are few incentives for federal officials to hold down the cost of construction. "In the direct federal construction programs," it observed, "the compensation of the professional employees involved is in no way related to the actual efficiency of the activity for which they are responsible. . . . There is simply no strong, clear reward system for efficiency in the federal construction programs."

Similarly, "there is very little incentive for the state and local governments which actually have the primary responsibility for executing design and construction to hold down costs, since most of these construction costs are in fact borne by the federal government.''

And then, of course, there are the sundry requirements, completely unrelated to efficient construction, which Congress has imposed on federal construction programs. The Commission asserts that environmental protection edicts, the Set-Aside Programs for small and small/disadvantaged businesses, the Buy American Act, and labor-protective statutes such as the Davis-Bacon Act, have combined to hamper "effective program management" and have "increased costs in a variety of ways.''

Another problem which undermines the attempt to hold down construction costs is the diffusion of authority and responsibility. "Currently," the Commission reports, "26 different agencies possess program authority to initiate construction. Many of these are relatively minor programs. Multiple construction programs, agencies performing construction for one another, multiple reviews of projects by nonconstruction agencies, multiple reviews within construction agencies, divided responsibilities in grant programs, restricted authority for quick decisions by resident engineers during construction, and Congressional involvement in key decisions have generated confusion and delays.'' The Commission found, not surprisingly, that "when everyone is responsible, no one is responsible, and decision making and cost control suffer.''

The Commission also found that "[i]ndividual projects and entire programs have become burdened with costly requirements yielding low or marginal benefits to the public as a whole . . . .'' These requirements have been initiated "in response to demands by groups, individuals, and other federal agencies, most of which have little or no responsibility for the success and cost of construction. One major result of these burdens imposed by Congress is a lengthy decision-making process which typically causes extremely costly delays and generates numerous wasteful design changes and repetitive review efforts.''

And what does all of this red tape mean? The Commission reaches the only logical conclusion: The government always pays more than the private sector.

Let us look at one of the major stumbling blocks: wage-setting legislation, and in particular, the Davis-Bacon Act.

The Grace Commission carefully scrutinized the three major prevailing federal wage laws and discovered that each presented a serious block to cutting the exorbitant cost of government.

The Davis-Bacon Act, which is the earliest of the prevailing wage laws, was adopted by Congress in 1931. As summarized by the Commission, it ''requires the Secretary of Labor to determine the 'prevailing wage' on federally funded and assisted construction projects.'' Davis-Bacon was originally intended to prevent unscrupulous outside contractors from bidding successfully on federal projects by importing cheap labor, thus undercutting local builders. But today, the Commission contends, the law ''is operated in direct contravention to its original purpose'' because it ''discriminates against smaller contractors, and has [anti-competitive] effects since it discourages quality contractors from bidding on public projects.'' In essence, Davis-Bacon removes wages and benefits as a factor in the competitive bidding process.

The Commission further found that Davis-Bacon, and related ''little Davis-Bacon'' laws which have been adopted by 37 states, ''raise the cost of public construction by a significant margin, in the range of $1 to $2 billion annually, or an average of $1.5 billion a year.'' The three-year savings without Davis-Bacon, the Commission speculates, would be $4.97 billion, which is slightly more than the federal individual income and employment taxes paid by residents of Alabama in 1982. The Act has outlived whatever usefulness it may have had, cannot be fairly and effectively administered, discriminates against small construction firms, and is costing the taxpayer billions in needless expense. The Grace Commission recommends that it be repealed.

The second prevailing wage measure, the Walsh-Healey Act, was signed into law by President Franklin D. Roosevelt in 1936. It applied to all federal contracts for the manufacture or furnishing of materials, supplies, articles or equipment which exceed $10,000. Persons employed on such contracts are to be paid no less than the minimum wages prevailing in the same locality for work of a similar nature, as determined by the Secretary of Labor. A 1964 court ruling took this wage-determination power away from the Labor Secretary, and Walsh-Healey is no longer an issue in that regard. Its practical impact today has to do with its requirements that overtime be paid for any work in excess of eight hours a day. This stricture effectively precludes the use of flexible work schedules — like the compressed 10-hour per day, four days per week arrangement — which have become popular in recent years. Those firms which operate with compressed workweeks for the convenience of their employees are discouraged from bidding on federal projects. This reduction in competition, combined with artificially inflated labor costs, led the Grace Commission to conclude that the Act should be repealed, to save taxpayers $3.37 billion over three years.

The third prevailing wage statute is the Service Contract Act. Enacted in 1965, it requires that employees working under federal service contracts valued at over $2,500 must be paid prevailing wages and benefits, as determined by the Secretary of Labor. The Grace Commission concluded that the Service Contract Act "needlessly raises the cost of service contracts to the federal government in the range of $500 million to $1.5 billion annually." For instance, the Commission noted the impact of the Service Contract Act on janitorial services: "In more than half of the G.S.A. [*General Services Administration*] Regional Headquarters cities . . . wage scales under federal janitorial service contracts are more than 20 percent above average commercial rates, usually because the established government rate approaches the union rate for the area. The average government rate equaled or exceeded the full union rate in three of those cities." It is that sort of thing, the Commission laments, which has "seriously limited cost-saving possibilities." Repeal of the Service Contract Act would save taxpayers $3.31 billion over three years.

The Commission found that the three wage-setting laws were having such an adverse impact on Air Force operations that "repeal or amendment of these outdated provisions could reduce construction and management costs by some $4.2 billion over three years, increase competition for Air Force contracts, and improve productivity." Undoubtedly, it would have that same basic impact on many other agencies as well, for the Commission concluded that repeal of the antiquated strictures could save taxpayers more than $11.6 billion. And *that* is only $1 billion less than the total 1981 federal individual income taxes paid by the combined residents of Kentucky, Tennessee, Alabama and Mississippi.

Construction

Once the buildings have been constructed, someone has to watch over them. The General Service Administration's Public Building Service (P.B.S.) employs 500 central administrators and 4,500 professional managers, at an annual cost of $125 million, to manage the properties for which G.S.A. is responsible. The individual agencies in the various buildings also have personnel assigned to this function. In comparison, the property management division of a major life insurance company handles a similar portfolio of properties, at approximately the same overall value, with only 300 management personnel and an annual cost of only *$9 million*! Other comparisons with the private-sector company revealed that "G.S.A.'s Public Building Service spends six times as much for inferior computerized information ($6 million versus $1 million)."

Attempts are being made, the Grace Committee reports, to reduce federal office space by some 19 percent per person. The problem is the typical snail's pace at which the bureaucrats are moving. Right now, the project is roaring along at the rate of 2.5 square feet per person per year. In perhaps 13 years, it may be completed. According to the Grace Commission: "The total potential savings for taxpayers comes to $11 million per foot reduction, or $350 million annually if and when this result actually occurs."

Don't hold your breath!

CHAPTER TWELVE
The Military

It is the mission of the Department of Defense and its subordinate divisions — Army, Air Force and Navy — to deter war and, if deterrence fails, to conclude any conflict on terms favorable to the United States.

While no sensible person wants to hamper the Armed Forces in performing this vital mission, the Grace Commission did find a number of areas ripe for potential savings throughout the Defense Department. The department has, for example, more than 5,000 installations and properties worldwide. Not all of these are necessary, and many are inefficient or uneconomical. Indeed, only 312 of roughly 4,000 installations in the United States are considered significant by the Department. (The others are support facilities with fewer than 150 employees each.) But over the last 20 years, many base-closing programs have been blocked by Congressmen from affected areas. For instance, of 17 military installations formally slated by the Department for closure since 1977, only three have been shut down. Congress has set up one legislative hurdle after another to make closing these unnecessary facilities wastefully expensive, time-consuming, and difficult. The Grace Commission notes, for instance, that one law requires "environmental impact studies for closing military installations." Each study "costs as much as $1 million." Some $2.7 billion could be saved over three years, if military installations were properly realigned and consolidated.

Cost overruns for military systems and spare parts have also become a scandal which has, unfortunately, tended to undermine the image of the military. According to the Grace Commission, cost estimates for 25 major weapons systems launched between 1971 and 1978 "have increased 223 percent — from $105 billion at the outset to $339 billion as of 1981 estimates." And why was that? The Commission explains: "Contractors for weapons typically 'underbid' to get a foot in the door, work then proceeds on the program and estimates are doubled and tripled. At that point in time, it's too late to stop the process."

Certainly, private contractors are at fault here. But so is the government, for failing to give private industry market incentives to cut costs. The Grace Commission says there is "insufficient financial incentive to industry to design lower-cost weapons systems. Contractors are given incentives to maximize quality and minimize lead time, rather than to reduce costs. As a result, in June of 1982 there were yet another 39 programs . . . identified as having cost estimating errors amounting to $10.8 billion, or about 9 percent of the original estimated costs."

One possible solution to this enormously expensive problem is "dual sourcing," or dividing the production of a weapons system between two contractors and awarding production quantities to whichever source supplies the best quality at the lowest cost. The Grace Commission describes it as "an effective method to introduce competition at both the prime and subcontractor levels."

Under the current system, once a manufacturer wins a military contract, perhaps by making an unrealistically low bid, that company becomes the sole source for 20 years, during which time costs (in the Commission's words) "are typically doubled and tripled in the absence of competition." If instead there were *two* competitive sources, however, the Commission estimates that annual savings of approximately $340 million would be realized in Navy operations alone. Dual-sourcing should be pursued, it advises, "when the quantities, rates, costs, and potential savings are appropriate to support more than one supplier."

Enormous price increases in spare parts for the Air Force and Navy have also been disclosed from recent audits. A few examples cited by the Commission: (a) a Minuteman II missile screw which cost $1.08 in 1982 shot up to $36.77 in 1983; (b) a supplier in Mississippi bought a gravity timer from the sole manufacturer for $11 and sold it to the Navy for $256, for a profit of 2,227 percent; (c) the Navy's Training Equipment Center in Orlando, Florida, paid $511 for lamps which actually cost 60 cents; and (d) the Navy paid $100 or more for aircraft simulator parts which cost a nickle. Such price gouging is serious indeed, considering that the Pentagon paid more than $1.2 billion for spare parts in 1982.

One method which might at least partially alleviate the problem, the Commission suggests, is to order a spare part (or parts) at the same time the production part is ordered. This would preclude paying a super-high price later on. "For example," the Commission comments, "combined purchasing to buy F/A-18 investment spares could reduce program costs by one-third, from $1.8 billion to $1.2 billion for a savings of $600 million."

Once again, we come to the commissary system, as we have elsewhere. Actual operating costs of the commissaries are difficult to calculate, due to the large number of indirect costs which are not charged to the system. "These unreported or 'hidden' costs," the Grace Commission observes, "are generally paid from funds appropriated for the operation of the base or support organization at which the commissary store is located. These hidden costs include maintenance of personnel files, procurement services, contract negotiation, computer operations, garbage collection, autovon telephones, and motor pools."

As noted in the chapter on "Congressional Roadblocks,"

Congress is the primary obstacle in the way of having the military commissaries entirely contracted out for operation by the private sector. The key strategy employed by the commissary lobby over the years to prevent change in the *status quo* has been to seek significant expansion of the potential beneficiaries eligible to shop at commissaries. The Grace Commission observes: "The more beneficiaries the more pressure and votes that can be brought to bear against those reformers seeking to save tax dollars." For instance, when the Commission began releasing its preliminary findings early in 1983, it recommended the elimination of taxpayer subsidies to commissaries to achieve cost savings. The reaction in the commissary special-interest group was explosive. The *Exchange and Commissary News* for August 15, 1983, editorialized: "It's time for this market to wake up and stop waiting for the House Armed Services Committee to constantly stop everything negative from becoming law. Our associations and key industry leaders must anticipate rather than react to head off moves to contract out or close the commissaries." In Congress, bills were introduced to: (1) expand the commissary lobby by opening commissary stores to all persons who have left the military and are entitled to retirement pay, but have not yet reached retirement age; (2) open commissaries to "former spouses" of military personnel; and most expansionist of all, (3) establish a test program for the use of commissary stores by military reservists. That move alone could bring another 950,000 new patrons into the commissary system. Contracting out the commissaries to the private sector could result in annual savings of $758 million. But it is unlikely to happen, unless and until we elect a Congress which will befriend — not bedevil — the beleaguered taxpayer.

Other potential savings areas targeted by the Grace Commission include:

Technical Manuals *(Potential Savings: $97,000)*. The Air Force makes modification kits to update military hardware available to foreign governments. The kits include technical manuals. At one Air Force Logistics Command, the Grace Commission reports, "it was found that foreign governments were charged only $.59 each for 377 technical manuals which cost over $3,770 to prepare. This is an average charge of $1.57 per publication where actual costs are a minimum of $10." The cost recovery deficit for 11,500 technical manuals produced since 1978 is $97,000. It doesn't seem like much — except perhaps, to the 44 median-income families whose total federal income tax in 1983 was taken to pay the bill.

Fuel-Conserving Take-Offs *(Potential Savings: $1.2 billion over three years)*. The Defense Department used 7.5 billion gallons of petroleum in Fiscal Year 1981, which tallies out at roughly two percent of total U.S. demand and 80 percent of the federal government's total usage. That same year, the Department expended $5.7 billion for aviation fuel alone. The Grace Commission commented: "Despite the magnitude of these expenses, D.O.D. does not have an aircraft thrust/power management program, i.e., a fuel conservation plan achieved by reducing power on take-offs, trimming back engine speed to specifications, etc." In addition, the Department's fuel consumption has increased since 1979 *despite* a Defense Audit Service report recommending improvements which the Grace Commission asserts "could have saved $200 million annually." For eight major aircraft used in the Navy and Air Force, average fuel consumption per flight hour actually jumped by 3.3 percent between Fiscal Years 1978 and 1981. The Grace Commission states that the Department "could save

$1.2 billion over three years in fuel and engine maintenance costs by pursuing an effective thrust/power management program."

Jumping the Gun. On occasion, the Army has been known to lease property that is not yet ready for occupancy. As a result, it pays rent while a building is being renovated for usage. The Grace Commission, for example, cites an instance when "the Army Corps of Engineers leased the International Tower Building at the Baltimore-Washington Airport in Maryland on an "as-is" basis and could not fully occupy the building until some 15 months afterward. The apparently wasted rental payments and maintenance charges during the 15-month period totalled $0.6 million."

Dual Pay for Active Reserve Duty *(Potential Savings: $66 million over three years).* Many private-sector employees belong either to the Air Force or Air National Guard. When on active duty with their Guard units, three-fourths are paid by their employers the difference between their regular pay and the amount they receive from the Guard. The total, in other words, is equivalent to the paycheck they receive from their regular jobs. Federal employees, on the other hand, receive full regular pay in addition to their active-duty compensation. Changing the system to the standard private-sector policy would save taxpayers $66 million over three years.

Bonuses *(Potential Savings: $81.6 million).* In July of 1981, the Navy and Marine Corps launched a program, approved by Congress, to help solve aviator shortages by awarding bonuses to aviation officers. The Grace Commission found evidence that much of the bonus money — perhaps as much as $81.6 million of the $102.9 million appropriated for the program — is being squandered unnecessarily. For example, the Commission learned that

$27.9 million had been expended on Navy pilots who were "beyond critical retention years"; $28.7 million went to Naval Flight Officers, a specialty for which there are minimal retention problems and no critical shortage; and $25 million was given to Marine Corps pilots and Naval Flight Officers at a grade level at which there was actually a *surplus* of personnel. The bonus concept has merit, but not if 80 percent of the funds are wasted!

Competitive Bids *(Potential Savings: $70 million over three years).* When military personnel are transferred to assignments outside North America, the Military Traffic Management Command (M.T.M.C.) usually solicits competitive bids from private contractors for moving household goods. However, when the move is to either Alaska or Hawaii, competitive bidding is prohibited. This despite the results of a study, conducted as long ago as 1977, indicating that competitive bidding reduced moving rates by 26 percent to Alaska and 20.5 percent to Hawaii. The Grace Commission asserts that competitive bids for the movement of household goods to Alaska and Hawaii could save $70 million over three years.

The Coast Guard *(Potential Savings: $2.8 billion over three years).* In peacetime the Coast Guard is technically a branch of the Treasury Department, while during a war it acts as part of the Navy. But it is convenient to include a discussion of it in our chapter on the military.

The Coast Guard was launched in 1790, as a fleet of 10 cutters, to provide military-related (national defense) services to the American public. Due to its strategic position in relation to our shorelines and waterways, many additional responsibilities have been given to the Guard over the years. The Grace Commission believes that a number of those responsibilities ought to be privatized, or at least help pay for themselves through user fees.

For instance, of all the documented Search And Rescue cases, 80 percent occurred within three miles of shore and 72 percent involved recreational boats. Eighty percent of the cases involved non-emergency, non-life-threatening situations. The Grace Commission recommends that private-sector towing interests, which are sufficiently extensive and well-equipped to do the job, should be called on to handle non-life-threatening Search And Rescue incidents. And this is especially important since, in the Commission's words, "it was learned that the Coast Guard's costs are 12 times greater than those of the private sector when performing the same functions." The potential savings: $651.1 million over three years.

Commercial Vessel Safety (C.V.S.) is presently the Coast Guard's fifth-largest operating program. It consists of establishing, implementing and enforcing federal standards for vessels, Merchant Marine personnel, and other facilities engaged in commercial or scientific activity in our waters. A number of C.V.S. procedures are safety-related. But two non-safety-related activities are (1) vessel admeasurement (establishing gross and net tonnage of vessels to determine which statutes and regulations apply), and (2) vessel documentation (issuing various certificates and licenses). The Grace Commission recommends that both responsibilities be privatized, a move which would result in combined three-year savings of $130.7 million.

Short-Range Aids to Navigation (S.R.A.N.) is the Coast Guard's oldest operational mission. S.R.A.N. are markers placed in and adjacent to navigable waters under federal jurisdiction. Their main purposes are (a) to assist navigators in determining their position or charting a safe course, and (b) to warn of obstructions to navigation. There are four basic categories of work included in the S.R.A.N. program, two of which could clearly be privatized. One involves quick response to a navigational-aid failure, followed by light repair or replacement work. The other has to do with heavy-lift routine maintenance of the S.R.A.N.s. The Grace Commission recommends that both jobs be contracted out to the private sector, a move which would effect three-year savings of $477.6 million. That's about what the residents of Vermont paid in federal individual income taxes in 1981.

Currently, the entire Coast Guard budget comes from federal tax coffers. Yet, nearly one-half of the Guard's operating program services are provided to specific classes of marine users. As the Grace Commission observes, though "these activities have traditionally been subsidized by the Coast Guard, there is no inherent reason why the user charge principle cannot be extended to encompass these functions. These services are not being provided for the general public. Consequently, taxpayers should not be required to support them." The Commission recommends a user-fee schedule aimed at recovering all direct operating and support costs associated with providing services to identifiable users. Such services would include: (a) search and rescue efforts associated with non-life-threatening incidents; (b) short-range aids to navigation; (c) radio-navigational aids; (d) domestic icebreaking; (e) commercial vessel safety; (f) recreational boating safety; (g) port safety and security; (h) marine environmental protection; and (i) bridge administration. The Commission does *not* recommend user-fee cost recovery for: (a) search and rescue costs associated with life-threatening incidents; (b) enforcement of laws and treaties; (c) military preparedness; and (d) polar ice operations. "These activities have been excluded," the

Commission explains, "because they are services that benefit the general public and not a discrete marine user or group of users. Consequently, it is proper to support them with general revenues." But why should taxpayers give a free tow to the wealthy sportsman whose yacht runs out of gas?

The potential revenue enhancement from implementing a Coast Guard user fee is $1.6 billion over three years, an amount equal to the federal individual income and employment taxes paid by the residents of Idaho in 1982.

CHAPTER THIRTEEN
Data Processing

All federal functions are now dependent, to one degree or another, on the efficiency of Automated Data Processing (A.D.P.) systems. The federal A.D.P. network encompasses some 19,000 general purpose and special systems. Its work force of more than 250,000 people is about 45 percent more than the total employment roster of Exxon, the world's largest industrial company. Yet, the Grace Commission discovered that the government "is not spending its A.D.P. dollar effectively." In the early Sixties, the federal government was acknowledged to be the leader in employing state-of-the-art computers. By the mid-Sixties, it had fallen behind the private sector. And today, perhaps one-half of the federal A.D.P. inventory is so ancient that it is no longer supported by its manufacturers, and [must therefore] be maintained at great additional expense by specially-trained government personnel. Indeed, federal computers average 6.7 years old, which is twice the average for private-sector equipment. "As a result," the Grace Commission reports, "the Government maintains a special work force for the servicing, which pushes up the percentage of A.D.P. resources spent on personnel to 41 percent, versus an average of 36 percent in the private sector." And that difference costs taxpayers $1 billion over three years, an amount equal to the entire 1982 federal individual and employment tax burden on the citizens of Montana.

Obsolete computer systems within the Air Force are spewing out 500,000 pounds of paper each month. That adds up to six million pounds per year, enough to make a stack 33 miles high — the equivalent of 116 Empire State Buildings! "Modernizing this thoroughly antiquated system would save $580 million over three years," according to the Grace Commission.

The bureaucracy and red tape accompanying the government's computer acquisition efforts is also a problem. Whereas the private sector upgrades computers every two to three years, it takes from two-and-a-half to four years for the government simply to obtain a new computer!

The Commission also discovered that very little consideration is given to whether new computers are compatible (able to communicate) with those already in service. Some $12 billion annually is spent on computers, yet many cannot share vital data. For example, the income of transfer-program recipients is recorded in computers at the Internal Revenue Service, but the data cannot be matched with the eligibility requirements of such programs as compiled by the Department of Health and Human Services. "Thus," the Grace Commission asserts, "when one agency has information useful to another there is an information gap preventing the transfer of much data. This results in federal entitlement programs being routinely defrauded." In New York alone, the Commission reveals, "the regional office of H.H.S. [*Health and Human Services*] uses ten different kinds of incompatible computers."

Computer matching has been extremely successful in exposing fraud and abuse in government entitlement and loan programs, wherever it has been tried. For instance, the Grace Commission mentions that "a 1983 computer match of federal employee rolls and food stamp recipients performed by the U.S. Department of Agriculture (U.S.D.A.) Inspector General's Chicago audit staff resulted in the indictments of seven persons for illegally receiving approximately $126,142 in food stamps and welfare benefits in Cook County." And, three other persons were indicted in Lake County, Illinois on charges of receiving $84,534 in illegal food stamps and welfare benefits. On another occasion, the matching of delinquent student loans with federal employees revealed nearly 47,000 federal workers with more than 50,000 delinquent loans valued at $67.7 million.

But such efforts are isolated, and incompatibility remains the rule. The Grace Commission asserts that efforts "to improve this incompatibility are slow and insufficient." Compounding the problem "is the fact that no long-range planning for improving existing computer systems with state-of-the-art technology exists."

Additional signs of data-processing difficulties were uncovered by the Commission in such departments and agencies as:

Census Bureau *(Potential Savings: in the millions)*. It took the bureau more than three years to process data collected during the 1980 census, at a cost of $1.1 billion. Eighty-eight million questionnaires were *manually* checked. Editing of the questionnaires required the diligent efforts of some 37,000 clerks and a cost of $48.4 million — 45 percent over budget. At one point, the bureau decided to relax its editing tolerances to reduce the workload. "The use of A.D.P. technology to automate many of these operations," the Grace Commission asserted, "would reduce future census processing costs by millions through reduction in processing time."

Federal Aviation Administration. In 1976, the F.A.A. purchased approximately $4 million in data terminal equipment which, to this date, has never been deployed. According to the Grace Commission, the "equipment was ordered without a clear definition of its need or performance capabilities and was accepted before required testing could be completed. As a result, F.A.A. determined that equipment modifications were necessary to meet operational requirements." Those modifications have yet to be made!

Department of Transportation *(Potential Savings: $6 million a year)*. During Fiscal Year 1982, the D.O.T. contracted with the private sector for $18 million in commercial time-sharing services, despite the fact that 53 percent of its own computer capacity was idle during the prime operating hours of 6:00 a.m. to 6:00 p.m. (it was 80 percent idle the rest of the time). "This practice," the Grace Commission declares, "wastes $6 million of taxpayers' money per year."

Air Force Logistics Command *(Potential Savings: $579.8 million over three years)*. The A.F.L.C. is responsible for maintaining an inventory of some 900,000 items with a value of $24 billion. Modern automatic data processing equipment is vitally important to this effort, yet, during the past eight years the Command, says the Commission, "has let its computer systems deteriorate to the extent that they are now obsolete and not cost-effective." The Commission recommends an A.D.P. modernization program which, if implemented, could realize three-year cost savings of about $579.8 million. That equals the amount paid in federal income and Social Security taxes by 15,126 median-income families in 1983.

Social Security Administration *(Potential Savings: 8.5 billion over five years)*. Noting that private sector companies discovered long ago "that it is penny wise and pound foolish to skimp on salaries with computer experts," the Grace Commission chastised the Social Security Administration for ignoring this principle. The Administration is striving to modernize its computers and save money as well, so "only four of the 13 pay increases S.S.A. gave its computer people from 1971 to 1982 kept pace with those in the private sector. The result: massive turnover and therefore big delays getting the modernization program under way. . . . '' The Commission estimates that the delay will cost taxpayers $8.5 billion over five years — an amount equivalent to the total federal individual income tax paid by the residents of Wisconsin and Iowa in 1981.

Patent and Trademark Office. The 20,000 pieces of mail received each day at the Patent and Trademark Office are processed by an all-paper, hand-file and routing system. As a result, the Grace Commission asserts, the backlog of patent applications awaiting review is now two years, having doubled over the past six years.

Economic Development Administration. *(Potential Savings: $18.3 million over three years).* The E.D.A. administers more than ten different grant, loan, and loan-guarantee programs intended to help alleviate unemployment and assist families with low incomes. In 1981, the agency administered a portfolio of $1 billion, of which 41 percent represented delinquent business loans. According to the Grace Commission, the agency suffers from such a lack of adequate documentation ''for analyzing borrowers' economic health'' that a sizable number of its loans are unjustified. The result, the Commission asserts, is ''an appalling rate of bad loans and delinquencies.''

The Commission makes nine recommendations regarding debt collection practices at the E.D.A. which it confidently believes could, if properly implemented, generate combined savings and revenue enhancements totaling $18.3 million over three years.

Urban Mass Transportation Administration. *(Potential Savings: $163.6 million over three years).* An unusually revealing example of the problems spawned by out-dated or inappropriate A.D.P. systems was uncovered at the Urban Mass Transportation Administration. The U.M.T.A. provides financial aid, distributed through various grants, to municipalities and transit authorities throughout the country. It is the primary source of federal funding to help urban areas plan, develop, and improve comprehensive mass-transit systems. During Fiscal Year 1982, some 1,883 U.M.T.A. grants totaled $3.4 billion. A combination of General Accounting Office and Inspector General audits have revealed a number of serious problems. The G.A.O. reported, for instance, that "over $14 million in funds granted to the Massachusetts Bay Transit Authority was spent ineffectively, inefficiently, and uneconomically because of inadequate monitoring" by U.M.T.A.

The G.A.O. also charged that the agency "does not have accurate or reliable financial or project information because its computerized Management Information System (M.I.S.) is extremely limited and unreliable." The system, for instance, "cannot display funds carried over from a previous year or immediately update balances." As a result, sundry U.M.T.A. regional offices, and its headquarters as well, consider the M.I.S. to be so unstable that "each developed its own manual systems" — which, however, "are not consistent and do not comply with U.M.T.A. procedures.

When U.M.T.A. attempted to use its Management Information Service to compile a quarterly report in 1979, some half-a-billion dollars were left out. And the bizarre system, which has cost the taxpayer $10 million over the past several years, "contributed significantly to U.M.T.A.'s $1.7 million violation of the antideficiency statute," the G.A.O. reported.

The Grace Commission suggests that the time has come for the U.M.T.A. and its parent Department of Transportation to "make a commitment to design, develop, install and maintain a new computerized system." The annual savings would be $163.6 million over three years, an amount equal to the federal income and Social Security taxes paid in 1983 by 3,034 median-income American families.

The Grace Commission considers computer matching to be the government's "most cost-effective tool for verification or investigation in the prevention and detection of fraud, waste and abuse."

The Commission's Task Force on Automated Data Processing formulated 58 specific recommendations which, it reported, could result in three-year cost savings of more than $19 billion. Of that amount, $4 billion would result solely from up-grading existing systems or replacing them with current technology.

CHAPTER FOURTEEN
Veterans Administration

Defending the nation is one of the most important legitimate functions of the federal government, and most Americans would probably agree that those who have risked their lives for this country deserve our support. This is not to say, however, that we neglect even veterans' affairs when it comes to eliminating waste and curbing bureaucratic overspending.

As it happens, there is a substantial amount of sheer waste in the Veterans Administration. The V.A. administers a comprehensive system of benefits for veterans and their dependents, including compensation payments for military-related death or disability, pensions for certain disabled veterans and survivors, education, rehabilitation, home-loan guarantees, insurance, burial payments, and comprehensive medical care. The Grace Commission determined that $3.3 billion in cost savings could be made over three years, merely through increased efficiency. These savings would not — repeat *not* — affect the quality of benefits to deserving veterans.

For instance, we could realize savings of $82 million during the first year alone, merely by applying private-sector standards to the V.A.'s work-measurement system. An additional $450 million-plus could be saved by revamping the procedure the agency uses to identify and control erroneous payments. For instance, a routine computer match of V.A. benefit records by the Inspector General uncovered 5,815 cases where payments were apparently made to deceased beneficiaries. The V.A. was only able to confirm 256 of those cases, but even that small number represented the irresponsible waste of $1.2 million ($4,688 per deceased "beneficiary"). Similarly, the various educational institutions which enroll veterans are required periodically to report changes in enrollment status so that the V.A. can make accurate revisions of benefit payments. A combination of inefficiencies such as late reporting by the schools, the V.A. policy of making benefit payments for an entire school year instead of one term at a time, and inadequate V.A. procedures for detecting the excess payments, led the agency to make overpayments totalling $425 million as of January 21, 1982. Of this amount, it had recovered only $7 million (1.6 percent) since 1979. The Grace Commission speculates that, unless corrective action is taken, the V.A. will continue to make educational overpayments at the rate. of about $50 million per year.

Currently, the V.A. identifies over $500 million each year in overpayments (approximately three percent of total payments), but does not use the collected data to track down the *cause* of such errors. A proper analysis of the cause, the Grace Commission contends, could probably double (to six percent) the detected overpayment rate. If 90 percent of that additional $500 million could then be recovered, taxpayers would benefit by $450 million.

Other wasteful expenditures result from too much paperwork. Under the terms of a law passed by Congress in 1981, for example, the administrator of the V.A. is required to submit to Congress a detailed proposal for any administrative reorganization that affects ten percent or more of the permanent employees at a "covered office or facility." The stricture covers any V.A. office or facility that has 25 or more employees, or is a free-standing outpatient clinic. So, a reorganization involving as few as three employees (10 percent of 25) must be submitted for congressional review at least eight months before the changes are scheduled to take effect. The Grace Commission did not assign a specific savings figure to the repeal of this onerous requirement, but the worker-hours and paperwork involved represent a shameful waste of tax dollars.

Yet another $356 million in savings could be realized by improving management practices related to the V.A.'s mortgage-guarantee program. At present, for instance, the agency voluntarily acquires homes at foreclosure sales in 95 percent of the cases where a V.A.-guaranteed mortgage is defaulted. By the time such homes are resold, the V.A. loses an average of $6,700 per home due to sales commissions and property-management expenses. If the V.A. would simply honor the guarantee (which it has the option to do) and not purchase the homes, the savings would be substantial. During Fiscal Year 1983, for instance, *not* purchasing the 10,150 units projected to go into foreclosure could have saved $68 million.

Even when V.A. homes are eventually sold, the agency holds the mortgages for undetermined periods, a costly practice which, according to the Grace report, "subjects the government to the vagaries and risks of the financial markets, of which it need not be a part." If, instead, the V.A. were to package and sell such mortgages shortly after acquisition, the yield would likely be 90 cents for every mortgage dollar sold, rather than 58 cents as at present. "With average annual mortgage acquisitions of about $900 million," the Commission speculates, "it would follow that annual revenues of about $864 million are possible through our recommended program."

Then there is the V.A. hospital system. It was established in 1921 to meet the medical needs of veterans with service-connected disabilities. The massive number of casualties generated by World Wars I and II placed incredible burdens on the private hospital system. These burdens simply could not be adequately met without substantial federal involvement. That situation has changed dramatically today; for example, although the V.A. has no legal obligation to treat disabilities that are not connected with military service, *over 80 percent of the health care it renders today is for non-service-related disabilities.*

The manner in which V.A. hospital budgets are set tends to promote waste rather than curb it. For instance, budgets are allocated to the individual V.A. hospitals based on the number of patient-days each hospital records during the year. That means the more admissions a hospital gets, the more government money it receives. Naturally, this creates an incentive to increase admissions, and to delay discharges until another patient becomes available to fill a bed. Hospitals which fail to meet their targeted patient-day workload stand to lose a percentage of their budget appropriation.

The V.A.'s patient-treatment files presently lack key information on such matters as the names of attending physicians, details of a patient's condition, length of stay and reasons for hospitalization. With such information either missing or ill-defined, and practically inaccessible after it is stored, the V.A. cannot effectively plan a budget based on the typical "mix" of cases. Closing this "information gap" through improved automated data processing and other procedures could save $4.9 billion over three years, an amount roughly equivalent to the entire personal income tax borne by residents of Minnesota in 1982.

In addition, the V.A.'s accounting system does not reflect the actual cost of care. Itemized billings for each individual patient are not supplied, so rates are based on *average* costs, rather than *real* costs. There is no effective test to determine if veterans are able to pay for non-service-connected injuries. Often in such cases, a patient will have private insurance which could pay the bill, but authorities do not know about it. Appropriate improvements in these areas could lead to three-year savings of $1.4 billion.

The average stay in a V.A. hospital is 21 days — nearly three times the private-sector average of 7.2 days. It is a disparity which costs taxpayers $1.6 billion annually. It presently costs the V.A. from $100 to $140 to process — *not pay* — a single medical claim. The average among private insurance and other fiscal intermediaries is in the range of $3 to $6 per claim.

Another concern is the V.A. construction-administration staff, which consists of some 800 people. The private Hospital Corporation of America's construction program, of roughly equivalent size, is staffed by only 50 people. This 16-fold discrepancy means that administrative costs amount to eight percent of the V.A. construction budget, versus two percent in the private sector. Yet the average V.A. project takes seven years to complete, compared to two years for the private sector. Overall V.A. hospital construction costs range from 30 to 69 percent higher than those in the private sector.

It is the same with nursing homes, where the V.A. construction expense is $61,250 per bed, compared to $15,900 for Beverly Enterprises, a leading national private-sector nursing home operator. Whenever the V.A. runs short of nursing-home beds for veterans, it often contracts with the private sector for additional facilities. In Fiscal Year 1981, the average cost to the V.A. for such contracted care was $45 per day. But the cost incurred by the V.A. when using its *own* facilities for similar care was $109 of your tax dollars per day!

It is little wonder, in light of the available statistics, that the Grace Commission concluded the V.A. should phase out the construction of additional hospitals and stop construction plans for new nursing homes. Instead, the Commission recommended that the agency: (1) contract with private hospital companies to construct facilities according to performance specifications and lease them back to the V.A. (The V.A. would contract with private-sector firms to manage the hospitals); and (2) convert under-utilized acute care beds in its own hospitals to nursing-home beds, and contract with private nursing-home operators for any additional facilities which might be required. Such sensible adjustments of hospital and nursing-home policy would result in savings of $553.2 million and $391.8 million, respectively, over three years. The Grace Commission also recommends that the V.A. contract with the private sector for hospital management services at three hospitals on a trial basis, a move which would add another $95.3 million to the savings total. If successful, the private management concept could be adopted throughout the entire V.A. health-care system.

CHAPTER FIFTEEN
The Private Sector

The federal government — and the taxpayer — could save a lot of money by turning over more commercial services to the private sector.

Federal policy on the operation of commercial activities was first put forth by the Eisenhower Administration in a series of Budget Bulletins. In 1966, Circular A-76 was issued to establish guidelines for implementing the basic principle that government should not perform any activity that can be performed by the private sector. Or, as Office of Management and Budget (O.M.B.) Circular A-76 (Revised, March 29, 1979) put it: "The Government's business is not to be in business." Most recently, in August of 1983, further-revised Circular A-76, which attempts to establish a procedure for the review of commercial federal activities that could be handled by the private sector, declared: "In the process of governing, the Government should not compete with its citizens. The competitive enterprise system, characterized by individual freedom and initiative, is the primary source of national economic strength. In recognition of this principle, it has been and continues to be the general policy of the Government to rely on commercial sources to supply the products and services the Government needs."

But rhetoric is all we got. The actual implementation of that policy has been pathetic. The Grace Commission laments: "Twenty-nine years after the policy of reliance on the private sector for commercial services was first promulgated, there are an estimated 400,000 to 500,000 federal employees currently engaged in activities which could be performed at less cost by the private sector. Within the U.S. and its possessions, excluding the Postal Service, at least one out of every five Executive Branch civilian employees is performing a commercial function.

They are involved in an estimated 11,000 separate commercial activities, costing approximately $20 billion a year." Such being the case, the Commission is compelled to conclude: "The policy of reliance upon the private sector has been poorly implemented at best." The reason is simple: bureaucratic resistance.

The Commission contends that a major problem with government "is that it tried to do everything: food service, maintenance, laundry, fire fighting, etc." Such activities "consume major portions of departmental and agency budgets and work forces." One study showed that 11,700 such jobs in the Defense Department alone could be contracted out with annual savings of $70 million. If this policy were instituted throughout the government, as the Commission recommends, the three-year savings to taxpayers would be $1.2 billion, which is the amount of individual income tax paid by the citizens of New Mexico in 1981.

The Grace Commission reminds us that our federal government "easily ranks as the world's largest conglomerate," and is the nation's largest (a) power producer; (b) insurer, lender and borrower; (c) hospital-system operator; (c) landowner and tenant; (d) holder of grazing land and timberland; (e) owner of grain; and (f) warehouse operator, ship owner and truck-fleet operator. Much of this activity, the Commission contends, "represents interference in the private economy and an overstepping of the proper bounds of the federal government." It recommends that "billions of dollars in savings be achieved by returning many of these services to the private sector. . ." Specifically, it contends that *at least* $1 billion annually could be saved by contracting with the private sector for the government's commercial services.

The federal government reached its present bloated size

due in part to the misguided belief that it is the only entity capable of providing the services which citizens desire. "For example," the Grace Report recalls, "once the Government decided to provide the military with the benefit of less expensive food, it chose to implement this service by establishing a complete retail grocery system. In the 1860's, this may have been the Government's only option, but today this duplication of private sector services decreases efficiency for the military because management of the commissaries lacks the driving forces of marketplace competition. The Government, by directly producing the commissary service, creates a separate uncompetitive market with no pressure to control costs."

It's been the same in many other cases. The Commission cites such examples as *multi-purpose dams*, originally constructed in rural areas which "did not have investor-owned utilities to provide electricity"; the *Space Shuttle*, which supposedly involved financial requirements and risks beyond the scope of any private-sector firm; and *Veterans Administration hospitals* constructed in response to a shortage of facilities resulting from the large number of World War I and II veterans. Today, the need for government to run these services has declined or disappeared, as "investor-owned utilities that market electric power are commonplace; private-sector firms interested in space technology are anxious to provide capital for, and assume much of the risk of, space exploration; [*and*] investor-owned hospital corporations build and manage hospitals for a large variety of clients . . . " In each such case, the Commission points out, "an alternative implementation option to provide for the service currently exists. These alternatives are largely ignored by Government. Instead, Government competes with these businesses without regard either to the cost or the bottom line.''

Some of the inherent inefficiencies of government are compounded by policies which are incredibly counter-productive and contrary to sound economic thinking. Indeed, congressional budget policy can actually work to assure that an inefficient federal manager will be rewarded with higher appropriations and more staff, while a truly dedicated public servant is penalized. Why? Because a bureaucrat's record of red ink is likely to be excused on the grounds that he was understaffed and underfunded. Would a private-sector department head who lost money for his company be rewarded with more staff and funds? Unlikely. But an efficient administrator in the bureaucracy who, say, spends only 90 percent of his agency budget for the year, will most likely be perceived as running an *over*-funded operation, and may well see his appropriation for the next year slashed.

While the stated purpose of military commissaries is to purchase and resell food at the lowest possible cost, ''the managers' operating funds come from surcharge revenues, determined as a percentage of cost. Thus, the manager can increase the operating funds by paying a higher price for food.'' Notice that this system of incentives is exactly opposite to those in the private sector, where benefits lie in cutting costs and saving money, *not* in padding expenses and wasting budgets.

''Privatization'' enables government to *provide* a service without *producing* that service. Privatizing inevitably saves tax dollars, because it allows the incentives and flexibility of the competitive free market and natural flexibility to work. According to the Grace Commission, the ''chief benefit to be achieved is that marketplace incentives come into play, thereby promoting more efficient service delivery. Additional advantages include the potential of lowered cost and improved quality that result from supplier competition, the ability to make economic and performance comparisons when services are delivered both by Government and by the private sector, flexibility in choosing the size and mix of service, and less dependence on a single supplier.'' In sharp contrast, the Commission declares that government endeavors ''lack the driving forces of marketplace competition that promote operational efficiency in profit-oriented organizations.'' They often lack ''the management information systems that provide timely data'' on which effective economic decisions can be made. They can be (and often are) ''constrained by regulated 'safeguards' that inhibit a manager's freedom to manage,'' such as the regulations governing Civil Service pay and dismissal. The decision-making is commonly ''far removed from an activity.'' Government operations ''are often driven by 'political' considerations rather than efficiency considerations.'' Privatization, wherever it is employed throughout the government apparatus, works to overcome these deficiencies.

State and local governments, being closer to the voters and relatively restricted in their tax-and-spend options, have been more inclined to contract with private-sector firms for services than has the federal government. The Grace Commission cites a number of examples which demonstrate the savings potential of private-sector contracting. For instance, *Butte, Montana* contracted with a private firm to operate a municipal hospital. The annual savings were $600,000. *Newark, New Jersey* contracted out collection of one-third of its refuse to a private firm, producing annual savings of $200,000. *Orange County, California* contracts with a private firm to run its computer center. Annual savings: $1,600,000. *Newton, Massachusetts* contracts with a private firm for its ambulance and paramedic service; annual savings: $500,000. *Dallas, Texas* closed its late-night city-run gas pumping depots and authorized its police and fire department emergency vehicles to use the gasoline facilities at 7-11 stores after midnight. Savings were $200,000. And *Oakland, California* sold a museum and auditorium to private investors with a lease-back arrangement which assigns maintenance to the new owners; savings were a one-time $55 million revenue enhancement. Such examples are quite typical of the financial benefits (and usually an improvement in service) which many state and local governments are experiencing nationwide. What it took was the good sense to turn to the private sector for those goods and services which the free market produces best.

Whenever the *federal* government has contracted with the private sector for commercial goods and services, the taxpayer has almost always benefitted. For instance, during Fiscal Years 1979 to 1981, the Air Force contracted out 34 functions at a savings of $108 million. Subsequently, however, Congress imposed restrictions which precluded such "outside" procurements. The Grace Commission asserts that, if those restrictions were lifted, "taxpayers would be spared $333 million in unnecessary expenditures over three years."

Similarly, the Air Force has converted approximately 58,000 military positions to civilian positions since 1965. It also had plans to convert an additional 6,000 positions in 1982 and 1983, but disclosed that 4,200 of those positions could *not* be converted due to congressionally-imposed civilian ceiling constraints. The Grace Commission also reports that "Contracting out some 2,200 positions at three Strategic Air Command locations could reduce costs by $5 million annually.''

As in so many other areas where the taxpayer could save money, Congress is a major impediment to the widespread, beneficial application of the privatization principle throughout the federal bureaucracy. (See Chapter 19). For three decades, the legislature has balked at supporting even the semblance of a national policy relying on the private sector for commercial services. The Grace Commission cites instance after instance of congressional actions which have undermined, rather than enhanced, privatization. For example, the Fiscal Year 1984 Defense Authorization bill imposed a two-year moratorium on contracting out for fire-fighting and security services. As the Commission observed: ''Individual members of Congress are quick to become involved in decisions on whether to contract out a specific function at a specific location. Their intervention always has been on the side of the opposition to contracting out.'' This congressional resistance has a ripple effect throughout the bureaucracy. ''For example,'' the Grace Commission notes, ''federal managers are inhibited from taking actions to contract out, regardless of possible savings, if it means being subjected to pressures emanating from Congress. The attitude of the federal manager becomes why bother if he or she is placed at a personal risk of trouble and has nothing to gain personally by contracting out.''

In another instance described by the Commission, Congress deliberately held up for many months a contract intended to provide base operation services at a particular military installation, thereby precluding the savings which could have been realized during that time. Eventually, the contract was allowed to go into effect, and the same work formerly performed by 1,400 federal employees is being conducted by a private contractor using 1,100 employees. The General Accounting Office estimates that the contract will save taxpayers about $6 million annually. Officials at the installation report that the contractor is delivering better service than was delivered previously by the federal employees. Is your congressman supporting special interest groups which oppose privatization; or does he back the efficiency and economy of the free market? Ask him how he has voted on privatization.

The Grace Commission laments that programs "to increase the use of private sector commercial services have almost suffocated. *U.S. citizens each year are paying perhaps billions more than necessary, and receiving poorer service . . . by having their Government in the business of providing commercial service."* [Emphasis added].

This situation is likely to continue, unless and until the Congress is controlled by legislators dedicated to the free market and determined to privatize as many commercial government services as possible, for the good of us all.

By privatizing government programs in only eight areas, the Grace Commission asserts that savings and revenue enhancements totaling $28.4 billion can be realized. The changes would include withdrawing the federal government from the hydroelectric power business; involving the private sector in certain space-launching services (including a fifth Space Shuttle); phasing out the Veterans Administration construction program for hospitals and nursing homes, then contracting with the private sector for hospital and nursing home facilities and services; turning military commissaries over to the private sector where appropriate; selling the two metropolitan Washington airports to a local airport authority (today, Dulles and National are the only commercial airports in the country owned by the federal government); using private-sector options to improve the government's vehicle fleet; privatizing, or imposing user fees for, sundry Coast Guard activities (where lives are not threatened); and finally, employing the private sector to help solve the enormous data-processing problems experienced by the Social Security Administration.

There is endless potential for *improving* services while simultaneously cutting costs to the taxpayer. In 1982, for instance, an Inspector General's report concluded that a dozen Job Corps Centers operated by the Interior Department were "excessively costly," and that savings of $7.5 million could be realized by contracting their operations with the private sector. The Grace Commission itself noted that at Postal Service "facilities of 10,000 square feet or less, the average annual square foot cost for Postal custodians was about $1.88 as compared to $ .77 for contractors." The Commission cited a government study of three Postal Service regions, which revealed that private contracting for custodial services in those three regions alone could save $15 million a year.

To help identify as many other areas as possible within the federal apparatus which are appropriate for possible privatizing, the Commission recommends the creation of a "permanent review" structure to enable the government "to analyze each program for its privatization feasibility." A small staff would have "the responsibility for continuing, on a government-wide basis, the review of programs that could be transferred to the private sector and of placing new policies and programs directly in the private sector." Each federal agency "would be assigned the task of informing an office of privatization review of the specific, program-review opportunities."

CHAPTER SIXTEEN
User Fees

It is the formal (if largely neglected) policy of the federal government to conduct its activities in a business-like manner by, among other things, collecting user charges (fees) for its market-oriented or business-type transactions. The phrase "user charge" is defined by the Grace Commission as "any charge collected from recipients of Government goods, services, or other benefits which are not shared by the public and which provide a specific benefit to an identifiable recipient." It incorporates such revenue-enhancing mechanisms as *fees* collected to offset the cost of goods, services, or privileges supplied by the government; *prices* for the sale, lease, or other use of government property; and, *excise taxes* designed to recover the cost of government projects or services.

In 1966, there were more than 1,500 user-charge programs and, while no exact count is available today, the Office of Management and Budget (O.M.B.) speculates that there are about the same number at present. In 1982, $42.6 billion in user charges were collected government-wide. That is a mere fraction of the potential revenue from such charges, but it is somewhat encouraging. Yet, thanks to perplexing court decisions and unclear administrative policy, there remains much uncertainty and confusion in the Executive Branch regarding what fees can be collected under what circumstances.

In the transportation area, for example, user fees have been a key aspect of the Reagan Administration's attempt to rely more heavily on marketplace incentives. For many years, such fees have been the main support for federal highway construction and rehabilitation, bridge repair and replacement, and airport and airways operations.

The Grace Commission described the two most basic aspects of the user-fee principle: "One is fairness and equity in the distribution of the Federal tax burden. It is unfair to burden the general public with payments for a service that benefits only certain user groups.''

''The other principle relates to efficiency in the use of limited resources. When users pay for a Federal service they have an economic incentive to match the quantity and quality of the service with the cost of the service. In the absence of a user charge, the user has an incentive to request as high a level of service as possible, regardless of cost, since the cost is being paid by the general taxpayer.''

There are an enormous number of areas for potential savings to taxpayers through the imposition of user charges. When it comes to loan programs, for instance, the Commission recommends that the Farmers Home Administration (Fm.H.A.) ''collect loan application fees to recover the cost of credit reports on the applicants.'' *Potential three-year revenue: $23.2 million.* It urges that *all* federal lending agencies ''charge for loan origination, servicing and delinquency for direct loans.'' *Potential revenue: $2.9 billion.* The Rural Electrification Administration should collect loan-guarantee fees as well as direct-loan fees to recover its administrative costs. *Potential revenue: $43 million.* The Government National Mortgage Association should increase the portion of the service fees it retains to recover costs more fully. *Potential revenue: $21.6 million.* The federally-sponsored private banking agencies (Farm Credit System, Federal Home Loan Bank Board, Federal National Mortgage Association, and the Federal Home Loan Mortgage Corporation) should pay an increasing user charge each year for the money they raise, due to agency status, to better reflect the cost of money. *Potential revenue: $724.2 million.* Guaranteed student-loan fees should be increased to recover more of the costs of administration. *Potential* *revenue: $1.6 billion.* And Fm.H.A. and the Small Business Administration should impose ongoing loan guarantee fees to recover expenses. *Potential revenue: $85.4 million.*

The user-fee revenues proposed in the previous paragraph alone total $5,397,400,000, which "ain't hay." But it *is* roughly the amount paid in federal individual income tax by the taxpayers of Georgia in 1981.

The Commission discovered a substantial degree of confusion throughout the Executive Branch regarding what fees, charges, and prices should be collected for government products and services. Some of this problem has resulted from court decisions, as when the Supreme Court ruled in 1975 that the Federal Communications Commission (F.C.C.) could no longer base *all* of the fees it charges the communications community on the revenue which licensees are likely to realize. The agency remains free, however, to collect fees based solely on the cost of the services it renders to licensees, which is as it should be. It is estimated that the F.C.C. could recover about $40 million of its $80 million yearly obligation through such a cost-oriented fee schedule, but to do so would require a new cost-accounting system capable of providing the information required properly to retrieve appropriate fees. Such a system would cost approximately $5 million, but Congress has refused to appropriate the necessary funds. So, for lack of that $5 million investment, the F.C.C. has lost more than $300 million ($40 million annually) in cost-based user fees since 1976.

An alternative approach would be for Congress to impose a user-fee arrangement by statute (literally, it would be a tax). If instigated by Congress, rather than the F.C.C. itself, such a fee would not violate the 1975 Supreme Court edict. Legislation has been introduced in each Congress since 1976 to authorize such a legislated "user-fee," but no action has been taken to date.

Administrative policy — or lack of it — has also created confusion regarding user fees. The Commission discovered, for instance, that both the National Aeronautics and Space Administration (N.A.S.A.) and the Department of Defense (D.O.D.) maintain wind tunnels which may be used for research and development by the government and the private sector. But whereas the D.O.D. charges $6,000 per hour for use of its facility, N.A.S.A. charges only $2,000 per hour. It is N.A.S.A.'s position that certain indirect costs should not be included in its charges, whereas D.O.D. includes them. "The obvious result," the Commission notes, "is that private sector industries, as well as Government agencies, including D.O.D., overuse the N.A.S.A. facilities." Clearly, the Defense Department's interpretation is most in line with private-sector pricing principles and should be adopted by N.A.S.A. There is simply no justification for all taxpayers to subsidize the use of federal wind tunnels by a select few.

That is true in hundreds of other instances as well. For example:

Power Marketing Administration *(Potential Revenues: $4.5 billion).* The P.M.A.s include five Department of Energy agencies which administer federal power-generating facilities and sell surplus power to the public. However, as noted by the Commission, "Those served by the P.M.A.s are receiving a government benefit because the rate-making process does not effectively capture the allocated capital costs. The users have had the advantage of indirect use of federal funds at low rates and consequent low cost of power." Through a system of user fees established as part of the rate-making process, this benefit can be recompensed without depriving the users of access to power.'' The Commission proposes that the rates charged to P.M.A. customers be revised upward until they are at least one-half the cost of privately-generated power in the areas being served. It is a modest proposal indeed. Yet, the potential revenue recovery exceeds $4.5 billion, which is more than the $4.4 billion paid by residents of Kentucky in federal individual income and employment taxes in 1982.

Inland Waterways *(Potential Revenues: $600.7 million over three years).* For more than 20 years, the Federal Highway Program has been funded almost entirely by user charges based, primarily, on the fuel tax. Not so with the inland waterway system. Indeed, in Fiscal Year 1981, only $24 million of the $850 million expended for construction, operation, and maintenance of locks, dams, and channels which facilitate commercial traffic on inland waterways was recovered from user fees. That left 97 percent of the burden on the shoulders of taxpayers. The Grace Commission recommends modernizing the fee system to transfer a far greater share of the burden to those who actually use the system. Such a plan would generate an estimated three-year total of $600.7 million in new revenues.

National Park Service *(Potential Revenues: $66.2 million over three years).* During 1981 (the last year for which complete figures are available), the National Park Service (N.P.S.) operated 333 parks, yet charged entrance fees at only 64 of them. Total collections were $9.4 million from 298 million visitors. Compare that $9.4 million to the $452.7 million which Congress appropriated to operate and maintain the parks. Taxpayers are contributing an ever-increasing share, while park visitors in particular are paying a smaller share of park costs. Entry-fee revenues declined from seven percent of N.P.S. operation and maintenance costs in 1971 to approximately two percent of those costs in 1981, leaving taxpayers with *98 percent* of the burden. Visitors to the parks paid approximately three cents each in entrance fees, while each taxpayer donated $1.53 toward the operation and maintenance of the park sites.

Park fees presently range from $1 to $3 per vehicle and from $.50 to $1.50 for walk-in visitors. The Golden Eagle Passport is $10 per year, per vehicle, and authorizes admission to all national parks. Entrance fees at many state parks and private recreation facilities are at least twice as high.

The Grace Commission believes that those "who directly use and enjoy the Nation's parks ought to pay a larger share of the cost of operating and maintaining them." An additional $9.8 million in revenue could be generated by charging nominal fees at 23 parks for which entrance is now free; extending the hours of fee collection at 14 other sites; and increasing the Golden Eagle Passport from $10 to $25. At Grand Canyon National Park, for instance, a family of four in a single vehicle would pay $5 rather than the present $2. Keep in mind that this rate is still 44 percent less than the $8.85 charge for the same family to ride the elevator to the viewing deck of the Empire State Building.

In establishing appropriate fees at the different parks, such factors as level of demand, the number of accesses to the area, and the cost of necessary improvements could be taken into account. Net additional revenues during the first year could total $20 million (and $66.2 million over three years). User fees alone could never be expected to cover the *entire* cost of our parks, lest the parks become the exclusive domain of Smokey the Bear and the Rockefellers. But the Grace Commission's recommendations are a justified step in the right direction.

National Forest Service *(Potential Revenues: $371.6 million)*. The National Forest Service oversees 155 national forests, 19 national grasslands, and 18 land utilization projects located in 44 states, Puerto Rico, and the Virgin Islands.

The combined recreation appropriations for the service from 1978 through 1982 totaled $567.5 million, while the user-fee collections amounted to $93.4 million (or about 16 percent of the total). Taxpayers made up the difference. To increase that percentage, the Grace Commission recommends that the law be amended to allow the Forest Service to collect entrance fees, charge for annual entrance permits, and increase the number of camping and other special-use areas at which fees are collected. The Commission would also base ski-resort special land-use agreement fees on the value of the land (not on ski resort sales) and would change to a flat-rate rent basis. And finally, the Commission suggests that summer recreation homeowners on Forest Service land should be charged fees more in line with the current value of the land if it were sold. Revenues of $371.6 million could be gained from adoption of these policy changes.

Corps of Engineers *(Potential Revenues: $56.6 million over three years)*. The Corps of Engineers (Corps) administers one of the two largest federal systems of recreation. In terms of visitors, it includes over 4,500 recreation areas located within the 453 water projects the Corps manages. Yet, the agency is forbidden by law to charge entrance or admission fees to any of its water-resource recreation areas. It is also prohibited from charging any day-use fees at such areas, and is required to provide one free "primitive" campground at every campsite where fees are collected. Since it is limited to the collection of camping fees, the Corps retrieved only $8 million in recreational user fees during Fiscal Year 1982 (a meagre 6 percent of the costs associated with providing the services).

According to the Grace Commission, the Corps itself "estimates it can increase the total number of fee areas to 1,241 — almost twice the current number. By introducing a $2.00 entrance fee per private non-commercial vehicle, a $.50 fee for other means of entry, and an annual entrance pass available for $20.00, plus the user fees now being collected, the Corps estimates a total yearly revenue of $28 million, or about 3.5 times the current annual receipts of $8 million." Even when collection costs are deducted, the net revenues over three years would likely exceed $51 million.

The Commission recommends that Congress change existing law to (a) allow entrance fees to be charged at Corps recreation areas, (b) eliminate the requirement for free primitive camping areas where regular camping is permitted and fees are collected, and (c) allow day-use fees at Corps recreation areas. The Commission's estimate of new three-year revenues is $56.6 million — the amount paid in 1983 federal income taxes by 25,518 median-income families.

Deep-Draft Harbors and Channels (*Potential Revenues: $1.3 billion*). The Army Corps of Engineers spent $3.2 billion in 1981 to construct and maintain deep-draft harbors and channels for commercial vessels. Of that amount, a miniscule $38 million — about one percent — was recovered from user fees.

Similarly, the Corps assists the Tennessee Valley Authority in constructing and maintaining locks, dams and channels that facilitate commercial traffic on inland waterways. The Fiscal Year 1981 budget obligation for the two agencies was approximately $850 million, of which only $24 million (less than three percent) was collected from the waterway users. You, the taxpayer, paid the other 97 percent. The Grace Commission estimates that a user fee set to recover the costs of such services would generate revenues exceeding $1.3 billion.

Firewood *(Potential Revenues: $63.6 million over three years).* Prior to 1974, only persons living on or near forest banks could obtain permits to participate in the free-use firewood program. In 1972, for instance, only 64,000 free-use permits were issued and 200,000 cords of free firewood were removed. It was the energy shortage which prompted the Forest Service to provide free-use permits to anyone, so long as the wood they removed was for personal use. Between 1974 and 1980, free-use permits increased by 450 percent. In 1981, 900,000 permits were issued, allowing removal of 4.2 million cords of wood. It was an amount equivalent to 11.2 million barrels of oil priced at $30 per barrel: $336 million all told. The Forest Service now estimates that between the years 1986 and 2000, in some parts of the national forest network, the free firewood removal may exceed the annual programmed timber harvest.

As the Grace Commission points out, the Service "is providing a Government-owned product free of charge to identifiable beneficiaries." The Commission recommends that a minimum of $10 be charged for a firewood permit, plus an additional fee of at least $5 per cord. The new revenues generated by such user charges would total $63.6 million over three years.

Grazing Fees *(Potential Revenues: $76.1 million).* Livestock grazing is authorized and administered by the Bureau of Land Management on approximately 143 million acres of federal land in ten western states. Leasing or permit fees, which secure grazing rights on a particular lot of land, are the only revenue generated from public rangeland. However, such grazing fees do not nearly offset the costs of range-related activities. The Grace Commission reports, for instance, that in 1983 "estimated costs came to over $100 million, and fees were estimated at $18.5 million." Taxpayers in general were compelled to make up the difference. The Commission recommends that the Interior Secretary seek (and Congress approve) legislation to amend the Public Rangeland Improvement Act of 1978 so grazing fees may be increased to their fair market value. Potential three-year savings: $76.1 million.

The Forest Service also administers a grazing program encompassing 102 million acres of allotments in 36 states. In 1981, $34.3 million was appropriated for management of the program and grazing-fee receipts of $14.9 million (43.5 percent of budgeted spending) were collected. In 1969, an incredibly complicated formula was adopted for determining the comparative forage value of public lands versus private lands. From this it came up with an appropriate grazing fee. The formula results in different grazing fees each year. This compares with an estimated average market rate of $8.80 per Animal Unit Month (A.U.M.,) while western land sometimes runs as high as $14.00 per A.U.M. (An A.U.M. represents the amount of forage required to support one cow or five sheep for one month.)

The point, of course, is that the government is receiving less than fair market value for forage on the public rangelands administered by the Forest Service. In 1985, there will be an opportunity to review the present fee system and suggest changes. The Grace Commission recommends that either a more realistic fee formula be adopted, or that grazing rights be auctioned by sealed bid. It is estimated that the latter would double the average fees. The potential revenue enhancement from improving the fee structure is $49.3 million over three years.

"Free" Government Publications *(Potential Revenues: at least $80 million).* More than $1 billion in agency printing and publishing costs were taken from the pockets of taxpayers in Fiscal Year 1982, due to restrictions limiting an agency's authority to levy user fees for its publications. The Grace Commission notes that even a modest program of user fees could generate revenues of at least $80 million the first year.

Inspection and Grading *(Potential Revenues: $35.5 million over three years).* The federal government conducts numerous inspection and grading activities. Some are mandatory, such as meat inspection, and benefit the general public. But many others, such as meat grading and grain inspection, are voluntary and are performed by the government at the request of the user. The Grace Commission, believing that if "the activity is voluntary in nature, the user is receiving a benefit from the Government for which he should pay," recommends that user fees be collected for inspections in the latter category.

For instance, the Agricultural Marketing Service administers standardization, grading, inspection, market news, marketing orders, and regulatory and related programs for which user charges are collected from most of the beneficiaries. But Congress apparently played favorites by exempting certain areas from the user-charge requirements. These included marketing news for cotton and tobacco; applications for plant variety protection; cotton grading and warehouse inspection; and the services provided under the marketing agreements and orders program. The Grace Commission recommends that the necessary steps be taken to make it possible to apply user fees in those areas as well. These steps would generate $29.4 million over three years.

The Federal Grain Inspection Service (F.G.I.S.) is required, in the case of domestic grain marketed at inland locations, to make its inspections available on request and to recover the costs of the service from those who use it. Through mid-1982 (the last year for which figures were available to the Grace Commission) the revenues generated from the F.G.I.S. inspection programs were $21.6 million, while the costs of providing the service were $25.5 million. The Commission recommends that the service raise its fees annually to assure that 100 percent of its costs are recovered. At stake is an additional $6.1 million in revenues.

Freedom of Information Act *(Potential Revenues: $231.7 million over three years).* The Freedom of Information Act allows the public to request information from government files at little cost. If a request is deemed to be in the general public interest, all charges are often waived. And, even when there is a fee, it does not include the cost of reviewing the document to remove classified or privacy-related information. This is an important consideration since most of the time taken by F.O.I.A. requests is devoted to the review process.

There is a pervasive attitude throughout the bureaucracy that requesting information from government agencies is a valuable "right" of individuals, and that costs and charges should be given little or no serious thought. The fact that taxpayers also have the right to spend the money they earn as they choose, rather than be compelled to pay for the inquisitive inclinations of others, is often completely ignored.

Since the F.O.I.A. was signed into law in 1966, a number of so-called "service" companies (i.e., private-sector companies which file F.O.I.A. requests on behalf of individuals or companies for a fee) have sprung up. The fees they charge are frequently three to four times the cost charged by government agencies for the data they in turn sell. One company cited by the Grace Commission charges $24.50 as a processing fee for each request, plus 20 cents a page for copying, plus any agency charges incurred. In contrast, federal agencies charge (at the most) $5 per hour (divided proportionally for time spent) and $.10 a page for copying. Thus, the average costs of filing one F.O.I.A. request through a service company would be $59.50; through the government, $15.00. Needless to say, when the government neglects to collect the full cost of its labor and expenses in filling a service company request, the taxpayer makes up the difference, subsidizing the research on which the service companies rely for their success.

Between 1979 and 1981, 92 percent of requests for data under the Freedom of Information Act were subsidized by the taxpayer. In 1981, the Food and Drug Administration alone processed 33,200 F.O.I.A. requests, at a cost of $4.5 million, but collected only $231,000 in fees. This amounted to slightly over 5 percent of the total expense. Taxpayers covered the balance, although approximately 80 to 85 percent of those queries to the F.D.A. came from pharmaceutical-industry sources seeking information about competitors. (About 47 percent of the requests were submitted by service companies.) One drug company in Pennsylvania filed 563 F.O.I.A. requests during 1979. In 1982, that same firm filed 1,250 requests.

Of the 33,000 requests received in 1981 by the Food and Drug Administration alone, approximately 80 to 85 percent came from the pharmaceutical industry seeking information on competitors.

There might be nothing wrong with seeking information about one's competitors, or establishing a free-enterprise service company to assist with such requests. But those seeking such information should be required to pay for it. It is outrageous to force the taxpayer to pay for data supplied by the government.

The Grace Commission wants the government to stop playing F.O.I.A. favorites. It recommends that Congress pass legislation authorizing — and requiring — full cost recovery through user fees. The savings to taxpayers over three years would approximate $231.7 million.

Customs Service *(Potential Revenues: $363.5 million).* The Customs Service administers 53 functions, for which it is reimbursed through user charges. For instance, it receives an annually-adjusted fee for its "vessels and foreign domestic trade" activity. The fee is based on the time the customs officer spends performing the service and the rate of compensation which the officer normally receives. On the other hand, no such full-recovery user fee is applied to aircraft, for which the fee established by Congress is a maximum of $25. And even that fee can only be applied after normal working hours. During Fiscal Year 1981, $3.15 million was obligated for the Customs Service aviation activities. Under the existing fee system, $376,945 was collected during that year, a mere 12 percent of the servicing costs. A full-recovery charge would have generated an additional $2,773,005 in revenue paid by users, not taxpayers in general. And, in other instances, customs is neglecting to charge a fee at all.

The Grace Commission recommends that the necessary steps be taken to apply a user fee on commercial aircraft similar to that presently imposed on vessels, and that legislation be adopted to authorize the imposition of appropriate new or increased user fees in those instances where recipients of customs services are not paying the full costs. Projected three-year savings: $363.5 million.

* * *

The Grace Commission describes many other examples where user fees could generate significant revenues. The Agricultural Cooperative Marketing Service, for instance, could recover $4.9 million in revenue simply by charging user fees for its research and educational publications. The Commodity Futures Trading Commission could generate $37.7 million over three years by imposing a user fee on traders to recover costs. The Federal Railroad Administration could bring in $66.4 million in three years from broad-based system assessments to cover costs. The National Fertilizer Development Center of the T.V.A. could generate $83.8 million to cover its research costs by charging an appropriate user fee. And the National Oceanic and Atmospheric Administration could recover $21 million of *its* costs over three years by phasing in a full-recovery user fee to pay for the operation of the Mapping, Charting and Surveying Services Agency.

Elsewhere throughout the federal maze, the Interior Department could collect $410.4 million from increased user fees for outer continental-shelf minerals exploration and development. The Forest Service could increase its user fee for small-lot timber sales (possible savings: $99.3 million). The Metropolitan Washington Airports (Dulles and National) could increase landing and concession fees to generate an additional $57.6 million. And so it goes, in one instance after another.

In general, the Grace Commission recommends (1) that statute which authorizes the collection of user fees "should be amended to overcome the difficulties in administration created by court interpretations. This should serve to clarify when user charges should be imposed and minimize inconsistencies in application."; (2) that a centralized function "should be established within the Office of Management and Budget to identify opportunities for establishing or revising user charges; maintain sufficient information regarding costs in order to be able to recommend regular price adjustments as needed; and monitor comparable business activities to generate recommendations for program incentives and improvements"; and (3) that the pricing of government products and services "should incorporate standard economic and accounting principles, with prices reflecting both comparable market rates and also the full cost of producing the services and products." Implementation of the Commission's recommendations could generate revenue totaling $10.2 billion within three years. The wider employment of user fees is not just a more efficient way to generate revenues, it is much more fair. Those who voluntarily use commercial government services do not have the right to compel others to pay for them. The Grace Commission would restore respect for property rights to the sale of such services.

CHAPTER SEVENTEEN
Will It Never End?

Here are a few final examples of what Peter Grace and his team of fiscal ferrets uncovered while digging their way through the federal bureaucracy:

Reduction-In-Force Rip-off *(Potential Savings: $34 million)*. The Grace Commission estimates that at least 8,000 federal employees are being paid for jobs whose official grades are higher than their actual assignments. This is because "current reduction-in-force (R.I.F.) procedures provide that federal employees retain their previous salary grade for two years if they are reduced to a lower level position through no fault of their own." In the private sector there is no such rule; individuals are paid according to what their labor is worth in the free market. Incredibly, the Commission notes cases where government employees earning more than $40,000 have been reduced to clerical level, yet still receive their $40,000-plus salaries. Private companies could not survive by paying their clerks $40,000; but the government can do it, because *its* income comes from your tax dollars. Employees who are over-compensated under R.I.F. rules cost taxpayers $34 million in 1982.

Retirement Benefits *(Potential Savings: $314 billion over ten years)*. Civil Service Retirement System (C.S.R.S.) benefits are about three times as lucrative as those of the top private-sector plans. The military-retirement system benefits are about six times as high. The Grace Commission notes: "Virtually every provision of these two federal retirement systems is more costly than comparable provisions of the top private-sector plans. If Congress had instituted a federal C.S.R.S. equal to a typical plan in a Fortune 500 company instead of the currently existing plan, the two largest federal retirement systems would have saved the taxpayer $103 billion over the last ten years. In the next ten years, the taxpayer would save $314 billion" — equivalent to $1,330 for every presently-living man, woman, and child in the nation — "compared to what is obligated and certain to be spent if no changes are made."

The Grace Commission's key recommendations concerning the federal retirement system include the following: Amend the C.S.R.S. to raise the retirement age from 55 to 62; calculate retirement benefits based on the average salary over five years (instead of three); reduce pension benefits by 0.33 percent for each month of early retirement; remove disability provisions from the retirement system; base cost-of-living adjustments on average increases granted in the private sector; and, bring federal employees into the Social Security system (a move already achieved in the case of federal employees hired on or after January 1, 1984). The Commission also wants the government to amend the Military Retirement System in ways which would still leave it superior to the better private-sector plans. The Grace Commission believes our military personnel deserve superior benefits, due to the special nature of their calling. But the Commission's plan would also reduce the extremely high cost associated with the very early retirement that is characteristic of the armed forces. Officers in the military usually retire at about age 43, enlisteds at age 39. This is *not* to say that the federal government should renege on its existing contracts with military personnel. Indeed, we feel that the only reasonable plan would be to change the pension and retirement arrangements for those just entering the military service.

While there is not room here to discuss in detail all of the Commission's recommendations regarding federal retirement policy, we were impressed by the Commission's humane yet fiscally responsible approach to an issue which must be dealt with if we are to put this nation's fiscal house in order.

Small Business Administration Field Offices *(Potential Savings: $3.0 million over three years).* The S.B.A. has ten regional offices staffed by 500 people. Data compiled by the S.B.A. itself indicate an uneven work distribution among the regions. The Grace Commission recommends that Regions VII and VIII be merged, and the same for Regions IX and X. The new arrangement would not only reduce the number of regions to eight, but would allow a reduction in staff for each new region of 10 and 19, respectively, to stay in line with the other six regions. Three-year savings: $1.8 million.

The S.B.A. also operates 22 branch offices as subordinate units of its district offices. Four branch offices (Harrisburg, Pennsylvania; Wilmington, Delaware; South Bend, Indiana; and Fort Worth, Texas) are located within 100 miles of an S.B.A. district office. The Grace Commission suggests that closing these four branch offices "may be warranted, considering the proximity of district offices which are capable of serving these branch offices' clientele, and the extra costs associated with maintenance of separate offices." The three-year savings from such closure would total an estimated $1.2 million.

Small Business Administration Loans *(Potential Savings: $112 million).* The Small Business Administration provides assistance of various sorts to small businesses, supposedly to enhance the free-enterprise system. Under the so-called 7(a) program, the agency tenders both direct and guaranteed business loans. The S.B.A. is authorized to guarantee up to 90 percent of a loan, or $500,000, whichever is less. The Grace Commission suggests that, if the maximum guarantee percentage were lowered to 75 percent, "the banks would have more invested in each loan, producing improved quality of loans and a smaller percentage amount for which the S.B.A. [*read: taxpayer*] would ultimately be liable." The Commission also recommends that *direct* lending by the S.B.A. be terminated completely in favor of guarantees: "If direct lending were eliminated, the loan making and servicing functions would become the responsibilities of the banks, and this would be more efficient for the S.B.A." — and the taxpayer. Reducing the maximum loan-guarantee percentage would generate three-year savings of $89.4 million, while dropping out of the direct-loan business would add another $22.6 million to the total.

Specifications *(Potential Savings: in the billions)*. The Grace Commission discovered that "Standard Federal Specifications," which specify exact materials for use in federal projects, "add billions to such projects." In contrast, the private sector uses less costly "Performance Specifications" to provide some flexibility while still achieving the desired result. According to the Commission, government's use of the stringent "Standard Federal Specifications," is wasting at least $400 million of each $20 billion in federal construction contracts alone — *a full 20 percent*! The total amount could have paid the 1983 federal income and Social Security taxes for 104,000 median-income American families.

Telephone Abuse *(Potential Savings: $13.1 million)*. The Grace Commission learned that long-distance telephone usage at the Department of Labor is virtually uncontrolled, with the result that costs associated with telephone usage have been escalating at ten percent or more each year for the past five years. And that is despite a *30*

111

percent decline in the total Department staffing over the past four years. Incredibly, one regional office of the Department reported that by restricting 95 percent of its telephones from commercial long distance, and reducing employee access to "Dial It" (i.e., Dial-A-Joke, Dial-The-Time, and Sports Phone), it had cut its commercial phone bill by approximately $1 million a year.

Unfortunately, such prudent steps have not been taken in most other Department offices. The Labor Department itself estimates that unauthorized calls account for between 10 and 40 percent of total calls made from within the Department.

A major problem, apparently, is that printed reports of long-distance calls made from within the Department are only done for the hours of 9:00 a.m. to 5:00 p.m. Since the reports are intended only to monitor usage trends, not to control costs, phone calls made before or after hours are not listed. The Grace Commission reported: "It is our understanding that D.O.L. employees are aware that their calls are not being recorded before or after this time frame, which may contribute to abuse before or after those hours." The Commission recommended that the Department implement a usage cost-control program aimed at reducing long-distance calls. It also suggested that the Secretary of Labor examine the feasibility and cost of securing 24-hour, 100 percent call detail as a more effective way to monitor long distance calls. The potential savings from both steps would total $8.2 million over three years.

The Grace Commission also discovered a massive glut of telephone equipment at the Labor Department. There has been a 30 percent decline in Department staffing in recent years. Yet, the purchase of telephone equipment has continued to escalate (multi-line telephones, regular telephones, adjunct telephone equipment, etc.) For instance, approximately 90 percent of the telephones at the D.O.L. are multi-line, compared to the 30 percent or less considered adequate in private industry. And, if you can believe it, the Commission learned that there are *more telephones than employees in the Department*! Whereas even a 1:1 ratio of telephones to employees is considered unusually high in the private sector, the ratio at the Department's national headquarters was 9:7 — nine phones for every seven employees. Even at the New York regional office, the ratio was 8:7. As a solution to this problem, the Grace Commission recommended that the amount and type of Department of Labor telephone equipment be reduced to conform with private industry and General Services Administration standards (which means cutting the percentage of multi-line equipment from 90 percent to no more than 30 percent of total equipment, and reducing the ratio of telephones to employees to at least 1:1, and preferably 4:5). The Commission would also reduce the Department's budget to reflect the potential savings of $4.9 million.

Tire Quality Grading *(Potential Savings: $3.3 million over three years).* The National Highway Traffic Safety Administration (N.H.T.S.A.) has been designated by government to promote highway safety by improving the crash-worthy performance of vehicles; encouraging safe driver and pedestrian behavior; informing consumers about the safety aspects of vehicle ownership, etc. The Uniform Tire Quality Grading System (U.T.Q.G.S.) is a N.H.T.S.A. program intended to provide consumers with comparative tire safety information regarding treadwear, traction, and temperature-resistance.

The cost to manufacturers to test for treadwear grades is about $10 million annually, yet the results of the tests vary to such a degree that even the Traffic Safety Administration admitted in 1982 that the standard could not be enforced. The temperature-resistance grade is of little or no value to consumers, since *all* tires, regardless of their Quality Grading System ratings, must · meet minimum safe-temperature requirements. So, in general, the Tire Quality Grading System has failed miserably to fulfill its legislative intent of aiding consumers in making passenger car tire purchases. And that failure has cost taxpayers $1 million annually in administrative costs, plus higher prices for tires as the tire industry passes along the costs imposed by the U.T.Q.G.S.

An evaluation of the U.T.Q.G.S. program by the Inspector General in 1982 revealed that most consumers are not aware of the existence of the program, and seldom use it in making tire-purchase decisions. The study also showed that the Grading System suffers from a serious credibility gap, due in part to the ludicrous nature of its treadwear grading operation. The Grace Commission firmly concluded that "U.T.Q.G.S. is an ineffective program because of technical infeasibility, lack of value to consumers and generally poor consumer and industry acceptance." It recommended that Congress promptly approve legislation cancelling the program, a move which would save taxpayers $3.3 million over three years.

Bureaucrats' Travel Costs *(Potential Savings: $993.3 million over three years).* Federal travel expenses totaled $4.8 billion during Fiscal Year 1982. Approximately 50 percent of that amount went for full-fare rates, despite the huge number of trips which should easily have qualified for substantial fare discounts. Can *you* afford to travel around the country with no attention to costs? The problem, the Grace Commission concluded, was the lack of centralized travel arrangements. The central purchase of travel tickets for all agencies, combined with the discount opportunities resulting from airline deregulation, would save taxpayers $984 million over three years.

Also, a substantial amount of governmental waste results from employee negligence in accounting for unused tickets. From 1976 to 1982, unused tickets valued at $17 million accumulated to the point where the General Services Administration was only able to negotiate refunds totaling $9 million. No settlement could be reached on the other $8 million worth of unused tickets, which represented the truly irresponsible waste of an amount equal to the federal income taxes paid in 1983 by over 3,600 American families. The Grace Commission asserts that, if "procedures were implemented to get government travelers to turn in their unused tickets promptly, taxpayers could be saved $9.3 million in needless waste over three years."

Vendor Performance *(Potential Savings: $60 million a year).* In many instances, it is cheaper for government to contract with private business to perform some services, rather than try to do everything itself. Unfortunately, the structure of government, which often protects special interests and relationships at the expense of good business practices, encourages abuse of the contracting system, both by private companies and by bureaucrats.

One major problem facing the system is a lack of communication. At present, for example, no centralized performance data is available on the vendors who supply the government. The lack of meaningful information concerning a vendor's past performance often means that different government agencies do repeat business with unsatisfactory suppliers. Even when one agency becomes aware of a vendor's unsatisfactory work, chances are quite good that the culprit will find a customer at some other agency. The Grace Commission speculates that the "extra costs incurred by repeat business with bad vendors are as high as $60 million *annually.*"

Weather Radio *(Potential Savings: $11 million over three years).* The National Weather Service (N.W.S.), a subdivision of the National Oceanic and Atmospheric Administration (N.O.A.A.), is responsible for meeting the nation's civilian weather-information needs in the interest of preserving lives and property and fostering commerce. Its Weather Radio program, launched in the early Sixties, provides a 24-hour continuous broadcast schedule to a national network of FM stations. That network currently consists of more than 367 stations covering about 90 percent of the population.

Is Weather Radio worth the approximately $8 million annual expense to taxpayers? The Grace Commission thinks not. After all, it notes, "Most people in this country have access to up-to-date weather information through radio and TV coverage." The Commission can "see no reason for N.O.A.A. to parallel this massive private effort with its own weather radio system." Indeed, even "recreational boaters, who seem to rely on . . . Weather Radio more than other segments of the public, have access to marine weather information from their local commercial radio stations or from an extensive network of Coast Guard and Navy transmitters." The fact that only a *very* small percentage of the population relies on the service makes it especially difficult to justify the expense. The Commission recommends that federal funding for Weather Radio be terminated. If phased out over a two-year period, the overall savings to taxpayers by the third year would be $11 million.

White Collar Imbalance *(Potential Savings: $4.8*

billion over three years). The federal government has 2.8 times the percentage of high-grade white-collar employees as is found in the private sector (72 percent versus 26 percent). Restructuring the federal workforce to parallel more closely the private sector could save $4.8 billion over three years. That's about what the residents of Hawaii paid in federal income and employment taxes for the years 1980, 1981, and 1982 combined!

* * *

And so it has gone, seemingly without end, in one aggravating instance after another of federal waste and mismanagement of our tax dollars. We must either unite as concerned taxpayers *and actively patriotic citizens to stop it,* or *we will likely be compelled to watch* as the strongest, freest, and most prosperous nation the world has ever known is brought to its knees in a quagmire of socialism and insolvency. In past generations, our forefathers have fought to preserve our freedom and prosperity. If our apathy allows that freedom to disappear, we will deserve the consequences!

CHAPTER EIGHTEEN
Truth In Budgeting

We must pause at this point to consider the outrageously misleading nature of the "official" federal budget. A basic recommendation of the Grace Commission is that *all* spending activity of the federal government, direct or indirect, should be candidly reflected in the budget. This is the only way for taxpayers to know what is actually being done with their hard-earned dollars.

Such honesty, however, is not popular among the spenders in Congress. They have developed ways to hide from taxpayers the true amount of government spending. Take the *offsetting receipts* ploy, for example. This spending subterfuge hides the true size of government expenditures by not counting in an agency's gross budget those funds generated from "business" transactions, like the sale of government property and products, loan repayments, rents, royalties for the use of federal land, etc. Of course, should the receipts stop coming in for some reason, the taxpayer would nevertheless be required to cover the agency's gross expenditures. Offsetting receipts for Fiscal Year 1984 are pegged at $330.5 billion — all now spent surreptitiously, as if this huge income didn't exist.

Congress also hides billions in *off-budget entities*, items for which tax money is obligated, but which are not included in the "official" budget. The first such departure from sound budget procedure occurred in August, 1971, when Congress excluded the Export-Import Bank from the budget. In subsequent years, the Postal Service Fund, the Rural Telephone Bank, and the Rural Electrification and Telephone Revolving Funds were withdrawn from the budget. And, from their inception, the Federal Financing Bank, the U.S. Railway Association, the Pension Benefit Guaranty Corporaton, the Synthetic Fuels Corporation, and the Strategic Petroleum Reserve Account were established as off-budget federal entities.

In the words of the Grace Commission: "[*If*] these entities operate at a deficit, their shortfall is covered by the U.S. Treasury, which borrows the money from the public — thus increasing the national debt. In short, having these entities off-budget misleads the public on the true magnitude of the federal government's spending, as well as permitting these entities to escape the normal scrutiny/limitation by Congress." Off-budget expenditures for Fiscal Year 1984 amount to $68.4 billion.

Unfunded pension liabilities are yet another obligation missing from the "official" budget. The "present value" of these future payments to cover such programs as Social Security, as well as civilian and military retirement and pension plans, was estimated by the Treasury Department to be $2.7 trillion on September 30, 1982. That equals the amount of money that would have to be set aside all at once today, in an account earning six percent annual interest, to assure payment of the promised benefits. For Fiscal Year 1984 alone, the minimal amount will be $202.8 billion.

The federal budget for Fiscal Year 1984, we are told, will entail outlays of $848.5 billion, which is surely bad enough. But when such factors as those described above are incorporated into the budget, the actual total of federal expenditures for the year *more than doubles,* to hit $1.8 trillion! That breaks down to more than $7,600 in tax payments for every man, woman and child in the nation.

With this in mind, let us now take a look at the Grace Commission findings which demonstrate the extent to which Congress, after approving deceptive budgets to camouflage the extent of its wild spending, has thrown one roadblock after another in the path of those who have attempted to curb wasteful spending.

CHAPTER NINETEEN
Congressional Roadblocks

Many Americans have wondered why it seems impossible to make even the most obvious cuts in wasteful government spending. The reason is: Congress. So intense are the pressures from special interests to spend, spend, spend, that Congress sometimes forgets to protect the taxpayers' interests. And taken separately, each little boondoggle seems to be just a drop in the bucket of the enormous federal deficit. So, by wasting $100,000 here and $100,000 there, we've reached a point where we have a pool of red ink amounting to more than *1.5 trillion!* That's why it is so important to start identifying — and eliminating — the giveaways bestowed upon aggressive lobbyists and special interests.

The Grace Commission described many instances in which congressional intervention either delayed or completely prevented spending cuts from being made. While Congress has the constitutional right to set funding levels for government programs, capitulation to pressure from special interest can make that right outrageously, and needlessly, expensive. Specifically, the Commission found that we could save about $7.8 billion over three years, plus an additional $1.1 billion in revenue generation, if the cost reductions now being hamstrung by Congress were implemented. Here are a few examples which indicate the nature and scope of this vexing problem:

Bookstores *(Potential Savings: millions each year).* Public printer Danford Sawyer wanted to close or consolidate 23 of the Government Printing Office's 27 regional bookstores. In 1981, the bookstores lost $9.7 million. Most are unpublicized and largely inaccessible in large cities (the Chicago outlet, for example, is on the 13th floor of a downtown federal building). Mr. Sawyer declared, "there's absolutely no need for them; 92 percent of our publications were sold by direct mail anyway.''

Bookstore employees promptly launched a lobbying effort (letters, petitions, etc.), directed at the Congressional Joint Committee on Printing. The committee approved a resolution rejecting any change in the bookstore *status quo* and forbidding Mr. Sawyer from tring to make other personnel changes to cut costs and curb waste. As the Grace Commission observed: ''There was a time, in the not too distant past, when Congress applauded rather than condemned public printers who took initiative to save the taxpayers' money. . . . Somewhere along the way, the attitude of Congress toward costs has changed.'' Indeed it has!

Bureau of Indian Affairs *(Potential Savings: $53 million over three years).* The Interior Department wanted to consolidate the 12 area offices of the Bureau of Indian Affairs (which administer programs on a region-wide basis) into five regional service centers and two special-services offices. The move would have saved taxpayers $16 million annually, and $53 million over three years. But it was scuttled by the obstructionist tactics of a member of the House Interior Appropriations Subcommittee.

Commissaries *(Potential Savings: $4.5 billion).* The system of military commissaries first evolved in the early part of the last century, when most army posts were generally located in isolated sections of the frontier. It was deemed reasonable at that time to provide our military men with food and other items at cost, partially to compensate for the unusually harsh conditions.

Obviously, the needs and conditions which originally justified the commissaries have changed dramatically. ''Harsh'' and ''remote'' conditions no longer apply to the 238 commissaries located within the continental United States. (There are 338 such stores worldwide, with 24,772 employees and annual sales exceeding $4.2 billion).

Unlike the self-sustaining post exchanges (which serve as military base "department stores" selling goods at wholesale prices), the commissary network depends on a taxpayer subsidy which totalled $758 million in direct and indirect costs in Fiscal Year 1983. As far back as 1953, the Senate Appropriations Committee reported: "The Committee fails to find any justification for the continuation of commissaries at military installations which are surrounded by or which abut metropolitan areas." In 1975, for example, at least six commissaries in the Washington, D.C. area were located within a three-mile radius of 88 major grocery outlets. Yet, when the Ford Administration made the modest proposal that year that the commissaries become self-supporting by Fiscal Year 1977, at least 15 bills and resolutions were introduced in Congress opposing *any changes whatsoever* in the commissary funding arrangement. The Administration's sensible plan was abandoned.

The Grace Commission notes that, since Fiscal Year 1977, "at least $3.2 billion in direct appropriated taxpayer costs have been incurred to subsidize commissaries. The indirect or 'hidden' costs to the taxpayer in that period…[run] about 42 percent of appropriated costs, or $1.3 billion. The grand total comes to *$4.5 billion that could have been saved* had Congress acted to place the commissary monopoly on an unprotected competitive footing in the marketplace." If the commissaries within the continental U.S. were contracted out to the private sector, the resulting savings over three years could total in excess of $2.5 billion. That's about what the taxpayers of Mississippi paid in federal individual income and employment taxes in 1982.

Consulates. During the Carter administration, the State

Department closed seven consulates in that many countries for budgetary reasons. Despite Department assurances that it could easily get along without the consulates, a senator and a representative decided they should be reopened. They succeeded in amending a State Department appropriations bill to direct that, beginning in Fiscal Year 1982, $400 million of the Department's funds be sent to reopen the seven consulates. Indeed, the language specified that until this was accomplished, no new U.S. consulates could be opened anywhere in the world! And, as noted by the Grace report, "The actual cost to taxpayers for reopening the consulates came to over $1 billion, as the building in Bremen, Germany, had already been sold, and a new consulate site had to be acquired."

Federal Information Center. The General Services Administration (G.S.A.) desired to close one of its Federal Information Centers and instead channel requests for government information through a toll-free telephone hotline. The move would have saved taxpayers thousands of dollars, but three senators and two representatives pressured G.S.A. into abandoning the cost-cutting plan.

Fish Hatcheries *(Potential savings: $10.9 million over three years)*. The Fish and Wildlife Service operates fish hatcheries throughout the nation, the output from which serves to restock streams, rivers, ponds, lakes, etc. As of 1982, there were 89 such hatcheries.

In 1983, the Interior Department proposed to close, or transfer to state management, 25 hatcheries on the grounds that they do "not contribute substantially" to major federal responsibilities in managing the nation's fishery resources. Department officials added that "in large measure the output of these hatcheries has been used to support...management of state-owned waters...and to stock farm ponds on private lands.'' The list of 25 hatcheries included five which had been proposed for closing in 1982, but which Congress had ordered to be continued for an additional year. Several of the remaining 20 had been proposed for closing in 1982, but Congress insisted on keeping them open indefinitely. In the end, Congress ordered that *all* the hatcheries be continued. The Grace Commission estimates that closing the 25 hatcheries on the Interior Department list would save taxpayers $10.9 million over three years.

Food Safety and Inspection Service *(Potential savings: $8.2 million over three years)*. When the Agriculture Department moved to close down 27 area offices of the Food Safety and Inspection Service that were no longer needed, as well as the training center, a member of the House Agricultural Appropriations Subcommittee intervened to save the training center (which happens to be located in his district). In the process, this move also preserved the 27 tax-wasting offices. Closing the stations and the training center could save taxpayers $8.2 million over three years.

Forest Service *(Potential savings: $3.3 million)*. Prior to 1972, Agriculture Department officials succeeded in closing eight Forest Service headquarters (thereby reducing the number nationwide to 122) and consolidating 124 ranger districts (cutting the total to 651). These prudent moves saved taxpayers millions of dollars. But, in 1972, the Agriculture Department sought to reorganize the Forest Service field structure by closing three regional offices. Such consolidations had reached the point where severance pay and the transfer of employees had been determined, when two senators intervened on behalf of Forest Service employees who did not wish to be transferred. The legislators succeeded in amending the Forest Service appropriation bill to forbid the expenditure of any money "to change the boundaries of any region, to abolish any region, to move or close any regional office" without the consent of both the House and Senate Committees on Agriculture and Appropriations — a virtually impossible hurdle. The restriction remains on the books to this day.

On another occasion, when the Reagan administration and the Forest Service attempted to close experimental research laboratories in three locations, Congress not only intervened to prohibit the closure, but it actually donated more than $1 million of your money for the three labs!

Military Bases *(Potential savings: $267 million).* Everyone appears to agree that at least *some* of the Defense Department's 5,000-plus installations and properties throughout the world are unnecessary, inefficient, and/or uneconomical. Yet, during the past two decades, numerous attempts to close unneeded bases have been blocked by congressmen representing the affected areas. The Grace Commission notes, for example, that "of 17 military installations formally slated by the Department of Defense for closure since 1977, only three have actually been shut down. Indeed, one base had been scheduled to be closed in 1964, 1970, 1978, and 1979;" D.O.D. finally announced in 1981 that this 121-year-old installation will retain active military status.

Offices for Black Lung Disease *(Potential savings: $120,000 per year).* A sharply decreasing work load has made obsolete at least 20 field stations handling Black Lung benefit claims. During the past two or three years, the Labor Department has considered reducing the number of such stations. But even before the Department could submit a formal proposal to Congress, a senator succeeded in adding language to the Department's budget for Fiscal Year 1983, directing "that the Department of Labor take no action to close Black Lung field offices.'' The cost to you, the taxpayer? Approximately $120,000 a year in sheer waste.

Printing Wages *(Potential savings: $62.9 million over three years).* The Joint Committee on Printing has defended and protected current wage scales for the Government Printing Office. Those wage levels average 42 percent higher than the scales for similar jobs elsewhere throughout the federal bureaucracy. ''For example,'' notes the Grace Commission, ''in 1983, journeymen G.P.O. proofreaders earned $30,252, while their counterparts in other Executive Branch agencies earned $12,473 — a difference of 143 percent.'' Bringing the wages of G.P.O. employees in line with their counterparts elsewhere in the federal government would result in a three-year savings of $62.9 million. That's equal to the federal income taxes paid by 28,359 median-income families in 1983.

Private Contracting *(Potential savings: $333 million over three years).* During Fiscal Years 1979-1981, the Air Force contracted out 34 functions to the private sector, thereby saving $108 million. Congressional restrictions adopted since that time, however, have effectively brought a halt to such outside procurements. If those restrictions are lifted, the Grace Commission reports, ''taxpayers would be spared $333 million in unnecessary expenditures over three years.'' That figure equals the federal income taxes paid by 150,000 median-income families in 1983.

Regional Information Sharing System (R.I.S.S.) *(Potential savings: $32.8 million over three years).* The R.I.S.S. programs, as described by the Grace Commission, ''were a state and local concept of sharing intelligence information concerning criminal activity between state and local jurisdictions.'' Funding for the programs had been provided by the Law Enforcement Assistance Administration prior to that agency's demise several years ago. The Justice Department decided, quite properly, that if the programs were indeed worthwhile, then state and local governments should be willing to help pay for them. Since they were *not* willing to do so, the Justice declined to assume the entire financial burden. However, a senator succeeded in inserting language into the Department's appropriation bill for Fiscal Year 1984 *forcing* it to spend $9.9 million on seven regional information programs. The Grace report concludes that terminating federal funding of R.I.S.S. would save taxpayers $32.8 million over three years.

Report: Expensive and Useless *(Potential savings: $280,000 a year)*. During each of the last four years, the General Accounting Office has recommended that Congress repeal its requirement for an annual report on Shut-in and Flaring Wells in the Outer-Continental Shelf. But Congress has refused to act. The Grace Commission notes that the Interior Department continues to produce the report, despite the fact that it "does not fulfill Congress' intent to determine whether off-shore operators are deliberately withholding production in anticipation of higher prices;" it "is less necessary in light of recent decontrol of domestic energy prices;" and, its "annual cost of $280,000 is not justified in view of the report's minimal value and could be better spent in other areas."

True, $280,000 is not much when compared to the total federal budget, but it *does* represent the income taxes paid by 125 median-income American families.

Rural Abandoned Mine Program *(Potential savings: $2 million over three years)*. The Office of Surface Mining wanted to handle projects of its Rural Abandoned Mine Program through a state grant mechanism which, as described by the Grace Commission, "would eliminate a layer of bureaucracy at the Soil Conservation Service in the Agriculture Department, where the program money is sent for disbursement.'' The savings were estimated at $2 million over three years. But a congressman succeeded in inserting language into the Fiscal Year 1984 appropriations bill scuttling this direct funding to the states.

Soil Conservation Service *(Potential savings: $579.5 million over three years).* In 1981, the S.C.S. tried to place a hold on new starts of erosion and flood control projects, while those already under way were reviewed by the Water Resources Council. Two executive orders supporting this move by the S.C.S. were issued by President Reagan, but the response of Congress was to *increase* funding for watershed and flood prevention operations by 50 percent over Administration requests (from $128.5 million to $192.5 million). Even worse, in the process a senator persuaded his colleagues to back an amendment permanently to exempt six watershed projects from review by the Water Resources Council. (Needless to say, two of the projects were in his own state.)

Since that time, Congress has directed the S.C.S. to add 50 new projects to its list, and has increased total funding by 55 percent over the Administration's request (for a total of $579.5 million through Fiscal Year 1983). That's an amount equal to total federal income tax paid by 261,271 median-income families in 1983.

Weather Stations *(Potential savings: $12.6 million over three years).* Officials at the National Oceanic and Atmospheric Administration (N.O.A.A.) have for many years sought to eliminate unneeded and obsolete weather stations. Congress rejected closure proposals in 1979 and 1980. None were submitted in 1981. In 1982, N.O.A.A. proposed to close 38 of the 234 local weather stations, each of which was manned by five or fewer employees, for a savings to taxpayers of $1.8 million. Congress agreed to close 18 of the lowest priority facilities (including one staffed by a single person whose regular working hours were nine-to-five, Monday through Friday). Largely due to the efforts of one congressman who was determined to keep the stations open, Congress later in the year reversed its decision to close the 18 stations, and instead provided $1.8 million to keep all 38 stations open. In 1983, N.O.A.A. tried once again by proposing to close a total of 63 stations and thereby save $3.8 million. Congress rejected the entire package. No closings were proposed for 1984.

If Congress would close the 63 stations on the 1983 N.O.A.A. list, the three-year savings are estimated to total $12.6 million.

Keep in mind that these instances of congressional irresponsibility are merely a sample from the much longer list provided by the Grace Commission report. In addition to replacing the big spenders with fiscal conservatives on election day, what can be done to overcome the refusal of so many congressmen to vote for modest cost-cutting proposals such as those catalogued by the Commission? One of the most potentially effective tools, assuming it is wielded by a president who is truly committed to trimming irresponsible federal spending, would be the line-item veto.

CHAPTER TWENTY
The Line-Item Veto

Presidential veto power is authorized by Article 1, Section 7, Paragraph 2 of the U.S. Constitution, which asserts in part: *"Every bill which shall have passed the House of Representatives and the Senate, shall, before it becomes a law, be presented to the President of the United States; if he approves, he shall sign it, but if not, he shall return it, with his objections, to that House in which it shall have originated."*

At the time the Constitution was drafted, the term "bill" had a far narrower meaning than it does today. The Grace Commission explains: "In the early stages of our government, each bill was concerned with a single, specific subject which had to be clearly identified in the title. During this period, a president could veto all the proposed legislation on a single subject by vetoing a 'bill'." In recent years, however, "Congress has enlarged the number and scope of unrelated subjects that together comprise a bill, until a single appropriations bill today may cover several unrelated departments, agencies and programs." And this, in turn, means that the president is often "deprived of the authority selectively to veto proposed legislation on a single subject."

To date, 43 of our 50 states have given their chief executives the authority to veto certain items in spending bills without rejecting the measures entirely. This procedure is known as a "line-item veto." States which have tried this indicate that line-item authority is a *very* useful and worthwhile tool for controlling excess spending and maintaining a balanced budget. There is no such authority at the federal level and, as a result, appropriations bills approved by Congress are "all-or-nothing" propositions. The president must either accept an entire bill or reject it; he has no power to accept or reject parts of it.

The Line-Item Veto

Without a line-item veto, the big spenders in Congress are often able to push their boondoggles through by attaching them to a bill as a legislative "rider." A rider consists of language added onto a bill which has no direct relation to the main thrust of the measure, and so merely "rides" along with it. An obnoxious "rider" or two (and sometimes more) attached to a crucial appropriations bill forces even a budget-conscious president either to approve the bill with its wasteful spending additions, or reject the main thrust of the bill, which he may favor. The president must either approve what he opposes (in order to avoid striking down the entire bill) or veto what he approves (as a way to scuttle the one or two items with which he firmly disagrees).

A fascinating, if somewhat bizarre, illustration of the effectiveness of a line-item veto in curbing irresponsible or unconstitutional spending occurred during the summer of 1983. President Reagan was unexpectedly given the opportunity to use a sort of *indirect* line-item veto. Here, briefly, are the details:

A supplemental appropriations bill was passed by Congress and signed into law by the president, despite Mr. Reagan's serious reservations regarding one unsavory provision. The federal government had brought a case to desegregate the school system in Chicago. A district court ordered the U.S. to ante up at least $14.6 million to meet expenses incurred by the Chicago Board of Education in carrying out a court-ordered desegregation edict. To assure that such expenses would be met, the court froze more than $250 million which Congress had appropriated for *other* programs in Chicago. Congress, rather than challenge the court's constitutionally-questionable ruling, meekly capitulated, appropriating $20 million as a source of compliance funds in order to free up the hostage $250 million. President Reagan, however, was convinced that the district court had acted unconstitutionally, using funds designated by Congress for purposes other than those authorized by Congress. The court had usurped legislative authority, the president contended, and should be challenged on that ground to release the $250 million.

Here was the classic "no line-item veto power" dilemma: the president either had to sign the bill, despite his reservations regarding one of its provisions, or veto the entire measure. He opted to sign.

But wait! Someone subsequently discovered that the distasteful provision had inadvertently been omitted from the official enrolled version of the bill. That being the case, it was necessary to submit that provision as a separate joint resolution, which Congress promptly passed, but which President Reagan vetoed. No attempt was made to override the veto, so the controversial appropriation was scuttled.

Many Americans mistakenly think it is the president who is primarily responsible for federal budget deficits. In fact, it is Congress which must accept the major responsibility in that regard. But a line-item veto would go far truly to balance the scales between the two. Today, the president has no authority to reduce the individual appropriations approved by Congress. The line-item veto would give him that authority, and thereby greatly increase his personal responsibility for the shape of the final budget. (Congress, of course, would have the same authority to override line-item vetoes as it now does to override all-or-nothing vetoes.)

It will probably require a constitutional amendment to legitimize the line-item veto. But the time and effort it may take to achieve that goal seems justified. The Grace Commission correctly concluded that important changes in our political processes should not be made unless doing so is of critical importance. "Thus," it explains, "in the 1960s it was possible to tolerate whatever inefficiency that legislative riders and similar actions introduced into administrative matters simply because the resulting budget deficits averaged a 'manageable' $6 billion a year. Now, however, the country is facing deficits approaching $200 billion annually." And the prospect that they will reach $2 *trillion* by the end of the century.

Just as the time for toleration of this continuing fiscal madness is long past, so the time for a line-item veto has come!

CHAPTER TWENTY-ONE
And So, Let's Do Something!

The Grace Commission contends that "the United States, as we enter the mid-1980's, is in a new ball-game — one where many of the old rules no longer apply. . . ." It is the Commission's view "that, if the taxpaying public were to realize how serious the condition of the federal government finances is, they would demand drastic action from their elected representatives."

As a taxpayer who has taken the time to become informed about the problem, what can *you* do to influence your elected officials and help others realize the crisis we face? The answer is: a lot. Here are a few suggestions:

1. Make the Grace Commission agenda a political issue in congressional campaigns. Ask those running for Congress in your state publicly to announce their position on the issue of cutting spending, and the proposals of the Grace Commission. Select one or two Commission recommendations which you feel strongly about and ask each candidate to declare his or her position on those proposals.

2. Raise the consciousness of your community by writing letters to the editors of newspapers and magazines; discussing Grace Commission recommendations on radio talk shows; and using every opportunity to bring the issue to the attention of friends, business associates, and others.

3. Purchase extra copies of this book, at the discount prices listed on the order form, for distribution to those who want to learn more. Then get a serious, knowledgeable group of concerned taxpayers together to confront your congressman at a town meeting.

4. Keep yourself well-informed and up-to-date on the issue of bloated government by reading books (and subscribing to periodicals) like those listed in Appendix A.

5. Contact your *state* legislators and ask them to support

legislation urging Congress to implement Grace Commission recommendations.

6. Urge President Reagan to establish a second private-sector survey similar to the Grace Commission, but this time devoted to scrutinizing the federal establishment to determine antiquated or detrimental laws which should be repealed, as well as federal agencies and activities which should be outright abolished. (Address: The President, The White House, Washington, D.C. 20500. Salutation: Dear Mr. President:) If the Grace Commission was "punch one," such a follow-up study could be "punch two" in a *very* effective one-two punch combination on behalf of limited, frugal government.

7. Know your congressman's voting record; has he voted to raise the federal debt ceiling? To hike spending for wasteful programs? To defeat a balanced budget? Let him know you are watching.

8. Peter Grace and the President's Private Sector Survey on Cost Control have established a toll-free number, 1-800-USA-DEBT. It will be used to mount a nationwide grassroots campaign to educate Americans about the Grace Commission's work and to make clear to Congress that taxpayers are fed up with wasteful government spending.

In a letter to the publisher of this book, J. Peter Grace wrote that authors Kennedy and Lee "are to be commended for your effort in helping us communicate the Grace Commission message to the American people. No matter how successful some may think our publicity and educational programs have been — working with television, radio, and printed media; social, civic, and business groups; as well as individual citizens; and our speakers bureau — there are still millions of American citizens who have never heard of the Grace Commission's work." Please call the Grace

Commission's toll-free number to find out how *you* can get involved in the Commission's efforts to restore sanity to our government budget.

Each of these proposals is a practical way individuals can make an impact on the November elections and on future government spending. If everyone reading this book did just one thing to help implement the Grace proposals, the impact on Congress would be overwhelming.

It's about time we *did* take action. After all, special interest groups have been making their views known — quite successfully — on Capitol Hill for many decades. It is time for the taxpayer to let Congress know who is in charge.

Remember, the preceding pages have described a mere fraction of the nearly 2,500 Grace proposals. And the Commission itself investigated only a small part of the federal monolith. The Grace Commission agenda can only be the beginning of a far larger effort to place our nation's fiscal house in order. But a commendable beginning it is!

The preface to the Commission's final report to the president asserts: "The ultimate impact of what we have proposed will depend on whether the American taxpayer can be persuaded that the problems are real and serious, the need for action pressing, the possibilities for reform promising, and the time for action at hand. If successful, then those same citizens can be depended upon to let their elected representatives and appointed officials know that 'business as usual' in the federal government can no longer be tolerated, and that rapid and extensive reforms must be instituted."

Let's get going!

APPENDIX
Task Forces

The following complete listing of PPSSCC Task Forces (and their co-chairmen), and the volumes which comprise the *Management Office Selected Issues Report*, also includes the dollar figure for the combined three-year savings and revenue enhancement opportunities reported by each:

DEPARTMENT OF AGRICULTURE — (Savings: $12,843,600,000)
Co-Chairs:
William B. Graham, Chairman, Baxter Travenol Laboratories, Inc.
William Wood Prince, President, F.H. Prince & Co., Inc.

DEPARTMENT OF THE AIR FORCE — (Savings: $27,603,700,000)
Co-Chairs:
James H. Evans, Chairman and Chief Executive Officer, Union Pacific Corporation.
Robert W. Galvin, Chairman and Chief Executive Officer, Motorola, Inc.
Paul F. Oreffice, President and Chief Executive Officer, Dow Chemical Co.

DEPARTMENT OF THE ARMY — (Savings: $13,400,300,000)
Co-Chairs:
Roger E. Birk, Chairman, President and Chief Executive Officer, Merrill Lynch & Co., Inc.
John L. Horan, Chairman, Merck & Co., Inc.
William A. Marguard, Chairman, President and Chief Executive Officer, American Standards, Inc.
Lewis T. Preston, Chairman, Morgan Guaranty Trust Co. of New York.

AUTOMATED DATA PROCESSING/OFFICE AUTOMATION — (Savings: $19,062,600,000)

Co-Chairs:

William Agee, former Chairman, Bendix Corp.

Joseph Alibrandi, President and Chief Executive Officer, Whittaker Corp.

Donald E. Procknow, President, Western Electric Co., Inc.

BOARDS/COMMISSIONS - BANKING — (Savings: $9,398,600,000)

Co-Chairs:

Fletcher L. Byrom, retired Chairman, Koppers Co, Inc.

John H. Tyler McConnell, Chairman and Chief Executive Officer, Delaware Trust Co.

Robert T. Powers, Chairman, Nalco Chemical Co.

BOARDS/COMMISSIONS - BUSINESS — (Savings: $3,295,600,000)

Co-Chairs:

George H. Dixon, President, First Bank System, Inc.

Edward Donley, Chairman and Chief Executive Officer, Air Products and Chemicals, Inc.

Robert A. Pritzker, President, The Marmon Group, Inc.

John M. Regan, Jr., Chairman and Chief Executive Officer, Marsh & McLennan Companies, Inc.

Thomas I. Storrs, Chairman, NCNB Corp.

Rawleigh Warner, Jr., Chairman and Chief Executive Officer, Mobil Corp.

DEPARTMENT OF COMMERCE — (Savings: $729,800,000)

Co-Chairs:

Amory Houghton, Jr., Chairman and Chief Executive Officer, Corning Glass Works.

Robert V. Van Fossan, Chairman and Chief Executive Officer, Mutual Benefit Life Insurance Co.

OFFICE OF THE SECRETARY OF DEFENSE — (Savings: $44,756,600,000)
Co-Chairs:

Robert A. Beck, Chairman and Chief Executive Officer, The Prudential Insurance Company of America.

Carter L. Burgess, Chairman, Executive Committee, Foreign Policy Association.

James E. Burke, Chairman and Chief Executive Officer, Johnson & Johnson.

Carl D. Covitz, President, Landmark Communities, Inc.

DEPARTMENT OF EDUCATION — (Savings: $2,827,800,000)
Co-Chairs:

Spencer F. Eccles, Chairman, President and Chief Executive Officer, First Security Corp.

Alfred H. Kingon, former editor in chief, Financial World Magazine.

Nathan R. Owen, Chairman and Chief Executive Officer, General Signal Corp.

Robert H. Willis, Chairman and President, Connecticut Natural Gas Corp.

DEPARTMENT OF ENERGY, THE FEDERAL ENERGY REGULATORY COMMISSION, AND THE NUCLEAR REGULATORY COMMISSION — (Savings: $4,080,500,000)
Co-Chairs:

John W. Hanley, Chairman and Chief Executive Officer, Monsanto Co.

Roger Milliken, President and Chief Executive Officer, Milliken & Co.

ENVIRONMENTAL PROTECTION AGENCY, SMALL BUSINESS ADMINISTRATION, AND FEDERAL EMERGENCY MANAGEMENT AGENCY — (Savings: $1,859,600,000)
Co-Chairs:

William H. Bricker, Chairman, President and Chief Executive Officer, Diamond Shamrock Corp.

Ben F. Love, Chief Executive Officer, Texas Commerce Bancshares, Inc.

FEDERAL CONSTRUCTION MANAGEMENT — (Savings: $5,446,000,000)
Co-Chairs:

Robert J. Buckley, Chairman and President, Allegheny International, Inc.

Raymond C. Foster, Chairman, President and Chief Executive Officer, Stone & Webster, Inc.

Melvyn N. Klein, President and Chief Executive Officer, Altamil Corp.

John W. Kluge, Chairman, President and Chief Executive Officer, Metromedia, Inc.

Frederick P. Rose, Chairman, Rose Associates, Inc.

Paul J. Schierl, President and Chief Executive Officer, Fort Howard Paper Co.

FEDERAL FEEDING — (Savings: $298,400,000)
Co-Chairs:

H.J. Cofer, Jr., President, Rich-SeaPak Corp.

Henry H. Henley, Jr., Chairman and Chief Executive Officer, Cluett, Peabody & Co., Inc.

Edward L. Hutton, President and Chief Executive Officer, Chemed Corp.

Carl Karcher, Chairman and Chief Executive Officer, Carl Karcher Enterprises, Inc.

Edward W. Whittemore, Chairman and Chief Executive Officer, American Brands, Inc.

FEDERAL HOSPITAL MANAGEMENT — (Savings: $11,912,500,000)
Co-Chairs:

Raymond A. Hay, President, LTV Corp.

William B. Johnson, Chairman, IC Industries, Inc.

James L. Ketelsen, Chairman and Chief Executive Officer, Tenneco, Inc.

Henry E. Simmons, M.D., National Director, Health Care Consulting Programs, Peat, Marwick, Mitchell & Co.

FEDERAL MANAGEMENT SYSTEMS — (Savings: none projected, due to far-reaching nature of recommendations)
Co-Chairs:

Joseph E. Connor, Jr., Senior Partner, Price Waterhouse.

Harry E. Figgie, Jr., Chairman and Chief Executive Officer, Figgie International, Inc.

John E. Fisher, Chairman, Nationwide Mutual Insurance, Co.

Daniel W. Lufkin, Chairman of the Finance Committee, Columbia Pictures Industries, Inc.

J. Paul Sticht, Chairman, R.J. Reynolds Industries, Inc.

FINANCIAL ASSET MANAGEMENT — (Savings:

141

$23,502,900,000)
Co-Chairs:

Edward W. Duffy, Chairman and Chief Executive Officer, Marine Midland Banks, Inc.

Wilson S. Johnson, Chairman, National Federation of Independent Businesses.

Edward B. Rust, President, State Farm Fire & Casualty Co.

DEPARTMENT OF HEALTH AND HUMAN SERVICES: DEPARTMENT MANAGEMENT, OFFICE OF HUMAN DEVELOPMENT SERVICES, ACTION — (Savings: $601,700,000)
Co-Chairs:

Michael D. Dingman, Chairman of the Board and Chief Executive Officer, Wheelabrator-Frye, Inc.

Forrest N. Shumway, Chairman of the Board and Chief Executive Officer, The Signal Companies, Inc.

DEPARTMENT OF HEALTH AND HUMAN SERVICES: THE PUBLIC HEALTH SERVICE AND THE HEALTH CARE FINANCING ADMINISTRATION — (Savings: $13,338,500,000)
Co-Chairs:

Samuel H. Armacost, President and Chief Executive Officer, Bank of America.

Edward L. Hennessy, Jr., Chairman, President and Chief Executive Officer, Allied Corp.

Charles J. Pilliod, Jr., Chairman and Chief Executive Officer, Goodyear Tire & Rubber Co.

DEPARTMENT OF HEALTH AND HUMAN SERVICES: SOCIAL SECURITY ADMINISTRATION —

(Savings: $9,387,000,000)
Co-Chairs:

John J. Byrne, Chairman, President and Chief Executive Officer, GEICO Corp.

Joseph P. Downer, Vice Chairman, Atlantic Richfield Co.

Harold A. Eckmann, Chairman and Chief Executive Officer, Atlantic Mutual Insurance Co.

George P. Jenkins, former Chairman and Chief Executive Officer, Metropolitan Life Insurance Co.

HOUSING AND URBAN DEVELOPMENT — (Savings: $2,817,800,000)
Co-Chairs:

Frank T. Cary, Chairman of the Executive Committee, IBM Corporation.

Richard Cooley, Chairman, President and Chief Executive Officer, Seattle First National Bank.

Barry F. Sullivan, Chairman and Chief Executive Officer, First National Bank of Chicago.

DEPARTMENT OF THE INTERIOR (Savings: $1,293,300,000)
Co-Chairs:

George D. Anderson, President, Anderson ZurMuehlen & Co.

William T. Coleman, Jr., Partner, O'Melveny & Myers

Morley P. Thompson, President, Baldwin-United Corp.

Hays T. Watkins, Chairman and Chief Executive Officer, CSX Corporation.

DEPARTMENT OF JUSTICE — (Savings: $850,100,000)
Co-Chairs:

Weston R. Christopherson, Chairman and Chief Executive Officer, Jewel Companies, Inc.

Frederick Deane, Chairman and Chief Executive Officer, Bank of Virginia.

Jewel S. Lafontant, Senior Partner, Lafontant, Wilkins, Jones & Ware, P.C.

Arthur Levitt, Jr., Chairman and Chief Executive Officer, American Stock Exchange, Inc.

DEPARTMENT OF LABOR — (Savings: $3,718,200,000)
Co-Chairs:

James S. Kemper, Jr., Chairman, Kemper Corporation.

Francis C. Rooney, Jr., Chief Executive Officer, Melville Corp.

Richard R. Shinn, Chairman and Chief Executive Officer, Metropolitan Life Insurance Co.

Luke G. Williams, Chief Executive Officer, American Sign & Indicator Corp.

LAND/FACILITIES/PERSONAL PROPERTY — (Savings: $626,900,000)
Co-Chairs:

John F. McGillicuddy, Chairman and Chief Executive Officer, Manufacturers Hanover Trust Co.

Donald G. McNeely, Chairman, Space Center, Inc.

Donald W. Nyrop, former Chief Executive Officer, Northwest Airlines, Inc.

Joseph J. Pinola, Chairman and Chief Executive Officer, First Interstate Bancorp.

Darwin E. Smith, Chairman and Chief Executive Officer, Kimberly-Clark Corp.

LOW INCOME STANDARDS AND BENEFITS — (Sav-

ings: $5,887,300,000)
Co-Chairs:

Bennett Archambault, Chief Executive Officer, Stewart-Warner Corp.

Richard J. Flamson, III, Chairman and Chief Executive Officer, Security Pacific National Bank.

Robert A. Schoellhorn, Chairman and Chief Executive Officer, Abbott Laboratories.

Robert K. Wilmouth, President and Chief Executive Officer, National Futures Association.

DEPARTMENT OF THE NAVY — (Savings: $7,185,000,000)
Co-Chairs:

Nicholas T. Camicia, Chairman and Chief Executive Officer, The Pittston Company.

Maurice R. Greenburg, President and Chief Executive Officer, American International Group, Inc.

Stanley Hiller, Jr., Chairman, Hiller Investment.

Thomas M. Macioce, President and Chief Executive Officer, Allied Stores Corp.

PERSONNEL MANAGEMENT — (Savings: $39,270,100,000)
Co-Chairs:

Robert Hatfield, President, New York Hospital.

Donald R. Keough, President, The Coca-Cola Company.

John A. Puelicher, Chairman and Chief Executive Officer, Marshall & Ilsley Corp.

PRIVATIZATION — (Savings: $28,417,100,000)
Co-Chairs:

Bruce J. Heim, Vice President, F. Eberstadt & Co., Inc.

Paul F. Hellmuth, retired Managing Partner, Hale & Dorr.

Edward L. Hutton, President and Chief Executive Officer, Chemed Corporation.

Paul E. Manheim, Advisory Director, Lehman Brothers, Kuhn, Loeb, Inc.

Eben W. Pyne, retired Senior Vice President, Citibank, N.A.

David L. Yunich, retired Vice Chairman, R.H. Macy & Co., Inc.

PROCUREMENT/CONTRACTS/INVENTORY MANAGEMENT — (Savings: $20,271,000,000)
Co-Chairs:

Willard C. Butcher, Chairman, The Chase Manhattan Bank, N.A.

Edward S. Finkelstein, Chairman and Chief Executive Officer, R.H. Macy & Co., Inc.

Clifton C. Garvin, Jr., Chief Executive Officer, Exxon Corp.

REAL PROPERTY MANAGEMENT — (Savings: $2,361,900,000)
Co-Chairs:

Robert A. Georgine, President, Building and Construction Trades Department, AFL—CIO.

Alexander F. Giacco, Chairman, President and Chief Executive Officer, Hercules, Inc.

Donald P. Kelly, Chairman, President and Chief Executive Officer, Esmark, Inc.

Donald B. Marron, Chairman and Chief Executive Officer, Paine-Webber, Inc.

Nathan Shapell, Chairman, Shapell Industries, Inc.

RESEARCH AND DEVELOPMENT — (Savings: $12,089,800,000)
Co-Chairs:
William F. Ballhaus, President, Beckman Instruments, Inc.
Karl D. Bays, Chairman and Chief Executive Officer, American Hospital Supply Corp.
James L. Ferguson, Chairman and Chief Executive Officer, General Foods Corp.
David Packard, Chairman of the Board, Hewlett-Packard Co.
Edson W. Spencer, Chairman and Chief Executive Officer, Honeywell, Inc.

DEPARTMENT OF STATE/AGENCY FOR INTERNATIONAL DEVELOPMENT/UNITED STATES INFORMATION AGENCY — (Savings: $742,800,000)
Co-Chairs:
J. Rawles Fulgham, retired Vice Chairman, InterFirst Corporation.
George L. Shinn, retired Chairman and Chief Executive Officer, First Boston Corp.

DEPARTMENT OF TRANSPORTATION — (Savings: $4,417,800,000)
Co-Chairs:
Coy G. Eklund, Chairman and Chief Executive Officer, The Equitable Life Assurance Society of the United States.
Thomas G. Pownall, Chairman and Chief Executive Officer, Martin Marietta Corp.
William H. Spoor, Chairman and Chief Executive Officer, Pillsbury, Co.
Terry Townsend, immediate Past Chairman, American

Society of Association Executives.
L. Stanton Williams, Chairman and Chief Executive Officer, PPG Industries, Inc.

DEPARTMENT OF THE TREASURY — (Savings: $11,506,300,000)
Co-Chairs:
Alfred Brittain, III, Chairman of the Board, Bankers Trust Company, Inc.
William H. Donaldson, Chairman, Donaldson Enterprises, Inc.
John H. Filer, Chairman and Chief Executive Officer, Aetna Life and Casualty Co.

USER CHARGES — (Savings: $10,210,900,000)
Co-Chairs:
James Stewart, retired Chairman, Frank B. Hall & Co, Inc.
Eugene J. Sullivan, Chairman and Chief Executive Officer, Borden, Inc.

VETERANS ADMINISTRATION — (Savings: $3,073,300,000)
Co-Chairs:
William C. Douce, President and Chief Executive Officer, Phillips Petroleum Co.
Hans W. Wanders, Chairman and Chief Operating Officer, Wachovia Corp.
William L. Wearly, Chairman of the Executive Committee, Ingersoll-Rand Co.

MANAGEMENT OFFICE SELECTED ISSUES REPORT

Volume I: PUBLISHING, PRINTING, REPRODUCTION, AND AUDIOVISUAL ACTIVITIES — (Savings: $1,727,800,000)

Volume II: TRAVEL AND TRAFFIC MANAGEMENT — (Savings: $1,850,000,000)

Volume III: FINANCIAL MANAGEMENT IN THE FEDERAL GOVERNMENT — (Savings: None projected)

Volume IV: WAGE SETTING LAWS: IMPACT ON THE FEDERAL GOVERNMENT — (Savings: $11,650,000,000)

Volume V: ANOMALIES IN THE FEDERAL WORK ENVIRONMENT — (Savings: None projected)

Volume VI: FEDERAL RETIREMENT SYSTEMS — (Savings: $58,100,000,000)

Volume VII: INFORMATION GAP IN THE FEDERAL GOVERNMENT — (Savings: None projected)

Volume VIII: THE COST OF CONGRESSIONAL ENCROACHMENT — (Savings: $8,825,300,000)

Volume IX: FEDERAL HEALTH CARE COSTS — (Savings: $28,900,000,000)

Volume X: OPPORTUNITIES BEYOND PPSS — (Savings: $15,947,200,000)

Volume XI: FEDERALLY SUBSIDIZED PROGRAMS — (Savings: $58,900,000,000)

Please note: Some task forces scrutinized issues involving more than one governmental agency. Inevitably, they identified certain savings which are also claimed by the agency-oriented task forces. Such duplication was found by the Commission to total $120,634,300,000. When that amount is deducted from the gross total of savings listed in the 47 separate Grace Commission reports ($544,985,600,000), the resulting *unduplicated* total of potential savings and revenue enhancements is $424,351,300,000.

QUANTITY DISCOUNTS

A Taxpayer Survey of the
Grace Commission Report

Give a copy to everyone you know!

Now is the time to pressure Congress to commit itself to the Grace Commission plan to cut federal extravagance and waste. Public pressure is the only thing that will do it. Order 20, 50, or 100 copies. Send them to your friends. Give them to business associates. Mail one to your senators and congressman. Make your office-holders tell you where they stand!

DISCOUNT SCHEDULE

1 copy	$ 1.95	100 copies	$ 85.00
5 copies	8.75	500 copies	100.00
10 copies	15.00	1,000 copies	500.00
25 copies	30.00	10,000 copies	3750.00
50 copies	50.00		

ORDER YOURS TODAY!

GREEN HILL PUBLISHERS, INC.
P.O. Box 738
Ottawa, IL 61350

Please send me postpaid _____ copies of A TAXPAYER SURVEY OF THE GRACE COMMISSION REPORT. Enclosed is a check or money order for _____.

Please charge my VISA ☐   MASTERCARD☐

Number_____ Expiration Date _____

Signature _____

Name _____

Street or box _____

City _____

State _____ Zip _____

(Illinois residents add 6% sales tax, please.)

3 1171